LIKE ANGELS ON JACOB'S LADDER

LIKE ANGELS ON JACOB'S LADDER

Abraham Abulafia, the Franciscans and Joachimism

Harvey J. Hames

State University of New York Press

Published by
State University of New York Press, Albany

Printed in the United States of America

For information, address State University of New York Press,
www.sunypress.edu

Production by Kelli W. Leroux
Marketing by Anne M. Valentine

Library of Congress Cataloging-in-Publication Data

Hames, Harvey J.
Like angels on Jacob's ladder : Abraham Abulafia, the Franciscans, and Joachimism / Harvey J. Hames.
p. cm.
Includes bibliographical references and index.
ISBN 978-0-7914-7271-2 (hardcover : alk. paper)
ISBN 978-0-7914-7272-9 (pbk. : alk. paper)
1. Abulafia, Abraham ben Samuel, 1240–ca. 1292. 2. Joachim, of Fiore, ca. 1132–1202.
3. Cabala—History. 4. Ecstasy (Judaism) 5. Salvation. 6. Judaism—Relation—Christianity. 7. History—Religious aspects—Christianity—History of doctrines—Middle Ages, 600–1500. I. Title.
BM526.H386 2008
296.8'2—dc22 2007014884

10 9 8 7 6 5 4 3 2 1

For
Mum and Dad
with love and gratitude

God's seal is truth.
—Babylonian Talmud, *Sanhedrin*

It is known that no intellectual should judge the work of another until one has read the whole book and understood everything therein to the smallest detail.
—Abraham Abulafia, *Sefer ha-Edut*

And it is the way of all authors who write books for the honour of God, everywhere and at all times; that he will no doubt suffer as a result of his book.
—Abraham Abulafia, *Hayei ha-Nefesh*

Contents

A Note to the Reader

Abraham Abulafia's hermeneutical style might seem rather daunting and incomprehensible. It is not easy, even for an experienced reader of Hebrew texts to study Abulafia, as, very often, the words that make up a sentence seem to make no sense. However, once one gets used to the way Abulafia thinks, then deciphering the meaning of the text becomes an interesting challenge and there is a feeling of achievement when what looks like utter gibberish suddenly takes on meaning.

For Abulafia, the letters of the Hebrew alphabet are the notes he uses to comprehend God, decipher the meaning of history, and predict future events. The Torah is the score that contains everything if one knows how to read, interpret, and hear it. Abulafia uses three main hermeneutical methods to reveal the true reading of the Torah: *Gematria, Temurah* (changing the order of the letters) and *tzerufei ottiyot* (letter combinations), and *Notrikon* (acrostics).

Gematria refers to the numerical value of the Hebrew letters of the alphabet. When words or phrases have the same numerical value, one can then equate between them, and learn about their secret meanings and connections.

The straightforward *gematria* starts from Aleph with a value of 1, Bet—2, Gimel—3, Dalet—4, Heh—5, Vav—6, Zayin—7, Het—8, Tet—9, Yud—10, Kaf—20, Lamed—30, Mem—40, Nun—50, Samech—60, 'Ayin—70, Peh—80, Tzaddi—90, Kuf—100, Resh—200, Shin—300, Taf—400. There are six final letters (meaning when the letter appears at the end of a word, it has a different written form): Final Kaf—500, Final Mem—600, Final Nun—700, Final Peh—800, Final Tzaddi—900. Hence, if one wants to use letters to represent a number, then, for example: 999 could be written Final Tzaddi, Tzaddi, Tet, or Taf, Taf, Kuf, Tzaddi, Tet. One thousand, however, can be represented by Aleph, two thousand by Bet, etc., hence the Jewish year 5767 in letters is Heh, Taf, Shin, Samech, Zayin.

There is also what is called *gematria ketanah* (little *gematria*)—this is when the letters from Yud and up (tens, and hundreds) lose their zeros and are counted as single digits. Hence, the *gematria* of the word *ha-kol* (All, Everything) in regular *gematria* is 55 (5+20+30), but in *gematria ketanah* is 10 (5+2+3).

The numerical value of words can also be worked out from the spelling out of the letters that make up the word and then calculating its value. For instance, *Bayit* (house) has the numerical value of 412, but also bet (*bet, yud, taf*) yud (*yud, vav, dalet*) taf (*taf, aleph, peh*) equaling 913.

A difference of one in numerical value between words or phrases is unimportant as one is omnipresent.

Temurah is essentially an anagram or the substitution of other letters for the original letters that make up the word according to systematic rules. For instance, an anagram of *Elohim* (one of the names of God) makes *male yah* (the plentitude of *YH*—another name of God and the first two letters of the Tetragrammaton) when the order of the letters is changed. *Temurah* can also be the substitution of one letter with another which is its equivalent in the order of the alphabet that is chosen. For instance, one of the most famous of these series is called *Atbash* which means that the first and last letter of the alphabet are interchangeable (Aleph—Taf), the second letter and the second from last (Bet—Shin), the third and the third last (Gimel—Resh), etc.

Temurah goes hand in hand with *tzerufei ottiyot*—letter combinations or permutations, which implies that the words of the Torah can be divided differently in order to get at their truest meaning and inner essence. The whole Torah is made up of letter combinations that imply that there is much scope for uncovering the permutations which allow one to discover the Divine names.

Notrikon is taking the letters of a word or the first or last letters of a series of words and forming from the letters a new word that has significant meaning or implications for the subject under discussion. For instance, the verse (Psalm 85:12) "*Emet Me-Eretz Tizmah*" (Truth will spring up from the ground) the first letters of each of the words form the word *EMeT* (truth).

Acknowledgments

This book started life as a lecture. In 2000, I was invited to take part in a group at the Institute for Advanced Studies in Jerusalem studying Apocalypticism and decided to present a paper on Abraham Abulafia and Joachim of Fiore. I had long suspected that there was a story to be told, and this was a perfect opportunity to present some of the material I had gathered. Following the seminar and encouraged by the comments of the participants, I started to write it up as an article. Due to other commitments, however, it was duly put aside. I returned to the topic at the start of my sabbatical year at Clare Hall, Cambridge, intending to finish the article and send it off and move on. Reading the paper again made me realize that there was much that needed to be fleshed out, and that there were major gaps in my argument. There is definitely something to be said for the "longue duree" when it comes to academic writing, and the result is what you are now holding in your hands.

It was the timely publication in 2001 of Robert Lerner's *Feast of St. Abraham: Medieval Millenarians and the Jews* which made this book easier to write. For a considerable period of time, I had been reading widely about Joachim and his Franciscan followers, but had felt a bit like the blind person trying to visualize an elephant by feeling it. I knew that there was something there and could feel the contours, but I lacked the necessary tools to conceptualize it. Lerner's book was a revelation! It felt a little like the elder Tobias having his sight restored, as in a wonderfully clear and concise manner, he set out the issues that aided in contextualizing Abraham Abulafia and clarifying much of what he did.

This study would have been almost impossible to write without the numerous books and articles on Abraham Abulafia and other aspects of Kabbalah by Moshe Idel. He is singlehandedly responsible for making Abulafia's Kabbalah comprehensible, and any serious student of the subject must start from Idel's textual analysis and presentation of Abulafia's corpus. While not always agreeing with my reading of Abulafia, Moshe Idel has always been willing to answer questions, tell me about new sources, and discuss the issues at hand.

It is always a pleasure to acknowledge those who helped this book along at different stages. Firstly, thanks go to Jeremy Cohen, Ora Limor, and Israel Yuval who invited me to join the group at the Institute for Advanced Studies. Other members of the fellowship listened, read, and commented on earlier drafts of this book. Particular thanks go to Alexander Patchovsky (who kindly sent me photocopies of the pseudo-Joachim commentaries on Isaiah and Jeremiah), Roberto Rusconi, and Bernard McGinn. My friend and colleague here in Beersheba, Elena Lourie, read the whole manuscript and in her usual amicable way, made incredibly insightful comments. Robert Lerner also agreed to read the manuscript and made important and astute comments as did Eve and Tony Bonner and Joan-Pau Rubiés. My sincere thanks to them all and any remaining errors are, naturally, mine.

Twice a year, a group of historians with different interests and nothing better to do, get together for a couple of days in Zichron Ya'akov, a small town in the foothills of the Carmel mountain range overlooking the Mediterranean. While enjoying each other's company, hearing good music, eating tasty food, and drinking good wines, these historians engage in intense reading and discussion of texts. The insights from those discussions are truly enlightening and the whole experience is uplifting. I had the pleasure of sharing some of the texts in this book with that incredible group of scholars and their penetrating comments and questions helped clarify some of the arguments presented here.

A picture is worth a thousand words, and being able to travel to Sicily and wander around Palermo and Messina also helped bring the subject of this book to life. Walking through what was the Jewish area in thirteenth-century Palermo and seeing the Franciscan church (built in the middle of that century) right next to the Jewish quarter made me realize just how difficult it would have been for Franciscans and Jews to avoid one another even if they had wanted to. Indeed, one could easily picture Abulafia making his way to the church, or standing in the narrow alleys around it deep in conversation with a friar holding a manuscript of the *Liber figurarum*.

I would also like to thank the people from SUNY Press, particularly Nancy Ellegate and Kelli Leroux, for their patience and perseverance. Authors are not always the easiest people to work with, and they made the whole process of bringing this book from manuscript to press enjoyable.

This book would probably have been completed sooner, had not my two daughters, Ya'ara and Talya, rightly demanded that I spend lots of time with them. They, together with my wife, Tiran, have incredibly enriched my life, and have taught me to put everything into perspective and recognize what is truly important. They both adore books and I hope that eventually, they will like this one as well, and consider the time away from them working on it well spent.

Introduction

Joachite eschatology had only marginal impact, if any, on the Kabbalistic forms of eschatology.
—M. Idel, *Messianic Mystics*

The title of this book is taken from a remark made by Abraham Abulafia (ca. 1240–1291) in the context of a disputation with a Christian, which can be seen as a central theme and thread that runs through his life, thought, and writing. Abulafia likened anyone seeking perfection and knowledge of the Divine intellect to the ascending and descending angels on Jacob's ladder. Each person, like the angels, is able to achieve the truth according to their capabilities and desire and some are closer than others to perfection. Abulafia saw himself as having reached the highest rung of the ladder and therefore, as chosen by God to reveal the Divine truth, concealed over time, because of the fast approaching end. These messianic aspirations, how they were conceived, developed, interpreted, and practiced are the focus of this book and they reveal a fascinating tale of fusion between Jewish and Christian apocalyptic ideas, which burst onto the historical stage at a particularly pregnant moment. A time of heightened expectation for some Christians who had adopted and adapted the teachings of a Calabrian abbot, Joachim of Fiore, and for Jews just entering the sixth millennium and hoping that it would signal the end of the exile and the start of the redemption.

Although this book focuses on a particular figure, the thirteenth-century Kabbalist Abraham Abulafia, it is primarily an attempt to show how ideas move between religions and cultures, and how permeable the boundaries erected between them are. Even in a society where there was no equality and the dominant faith influenced and limited the life of the minority faiths in many areas and diverse ways, there was still much scope for the exchange and interpenetration of ideas and this was not by any means one-way traffic. That there were contacts between the intellectuals of the three monotheistic faiths in the later Middle Ages is well documented. Christian scholars worked together with Jews and Muslims translating works from Arabic to Latin, sometimes also via Hebrew. Indeed, this translation activity was going on during Abulafia's lifetime in the courts of Frederick II and Charles of Anjou and some of the characters who appear in this book, such as Hillel ben Samuel of Verona, were involved, even translating Latin scholastic works into Hebrew. However, Abulafia's interaction with his Christian contemporaries was of a totally different nature. He adopted and adapted current Christian apocalyptic ideas, translated them into his own religious, historical, and moralistic world-view, and then repackaged them and tried to sell them back to his Jewish and Christian contemporaries.

Abulafia's works show that he was in constant dialogue with Christianity, or more precisely, with a mode of Christianity highly influenced by the thought of the twelfth-century Calabrian abbot, Joachim of Fiore. Some of the issues involved were intimately connected to the traditional and ongoing polemic between Christians and Jews. This debate had been growing in sophistication, scope, and ferocity since the twelfth century, and reached new heights in the thirteenth century with the trial and burning of the Talmud, the Barcelona Disputation of 1263, and Ramon Martí's enormous *Pugio fidei*. However, unlike many of his Jewish and Christian contemporaries who polemicized over eschatological themes, Abulafia focused on apocalypticism. Both he and his Joachimite contemporaries were convinced that the world was on the brink of a major change, the start of a new eon, and this made their polemic more immediate and vibrant because it was not dealing with questions that would be settled at some undetermined time in the future. The expected apocalypse was inevitable, was going to happen in the here and now, and therefore it was imperative for each side to show that the truth was with them. Abulafia sets out a counterhistory whereby the portrayal of Jesus, the Church, and the place of the Jews is the opposite of how they are depicted by Christians. He also gave himself a central role, as a serious challenger for the position of redeemer.[1] However, his polemic with Christianity and his very negative portrayal of this religion did not have a bearing on the place of Christians at the end of time, in the same manner that the Joachite portrayal of contemporary Jews, not significantly different from mainstream contemporary opinion, did not impinge on their positive inclusion at the end of days.

The focal point of Abulafia's interaction with Christians was the Franciscan Order, or the friars who adopted and adapted the teachings of Joachim of Fiore, and read St. Francis and themselves into his predictions regarding the period leading up to the third status. These friars who, by the middle of the thirteenth century, were to be found in places as diverse as Palermo, Paris, Narbonne, and Rome, read the genuine and pseudo-Joachimite treatises that they, along with the Florensians and Cistercians, contributed to, and saw themselves as one of the orders sent to lead the way into the age of the Holy Spirit. Abulafia's encounter with the friars would have taken place mainly in Sicily and southern Italy where he spent a considerable amount of time from the early 1260s, where he wrote most of his books, and where he conceived and developed his messianic expectations and apocalyptic framework. In his works, Abulafia mentions the Franciscans and it is this geographical location and historical context that gives life and meaning to much of what he did and wrote.

Abraham Abulafia has been the subject of attention by scholars from the mid-nineteenth-century onward. Moshe Landauer suggested that he was the author of the Zohar, and Heinreich Graetz wrote about Abulafia's life and mission.[2] Adolph Jellinek published a couple of Abulafia's letters and *Sefer ha-Ot* (Book of the Sign), his most famous prophetic work, and set the record straight differentiating between Abulafia's Kabbalistic system and the Zohar.[3] In his majestic survey of the field of Jewish mysticism published in 1941, Gershom Scholem devoted a whole chapter to Abulafia and ecstatic Kabbalah, though it is notable that aside from part of a lecture series delivered at the Hebrew University and an article in the *Encyclopaedia Judaica,* Abulafia was otherwise ignored by that doyen of the field.[4] It was Moshe Idel, starting with his doctoral thesis and then in a large number of articles and books, who really came to grips with Abulafia's Kabbalah and its central place in the development of Jewish mysticism from the Middle Ages onward.[5] Idel's groundbreaking work, based on the study of hundreds of manuscripts containing material connected with ecstatic Kabbalah, is now the focal point for all students of Abulafia and the field. In addition, Elliot Wolfson has written an important study which takes a different stance on some of Abulafia's central teachings, particularly regarding his attitude toward the Sefirot and the commandments.[6]

While Gershom Scholem studied Kabbalah from a historical-philological perspective, he did this essentially in order to recover the subterranean currents that were, in his opinion, always present in the Jewish tradition and which revitalized it. He referred to Jewish history as an internal dialectic of contradictory forces, and those undercurrents as emerging from within it, with little or no external influences. Hence, his approach to apocalypticism and messianism, which he saw as predominantly part of the mystical tradition, was as something inherently Jewish.[7] After Scholem, the methodology adopted for studying the texts of medieval Kabbalah has been primarily phenomenological. This places more importance on ideas and their transmission to other texts than in the historical context of the authors and their ideas. This means that while Abulafia is recognized as a major figure in the field of Kabbalah, and his teachings and methods resonate in the writings of later Kabbalists, the historical context of his works have not been closely examined. His place as the founder of the ecstatic school of Kabbalah and his influence on subsequent generations of Kabbalists in Spain, Italy, Safed, and elsewhere has been well attested, yet, the milieu in which he lived and developed his teachings is, surprisingly, almost totally ignored (one example being the opening quotation of this Introduction). The historical-contextual issue is compounded by another fascinating element. Almost from his immediate students onward, the apocalyptic-messianic elements of Abulafia's life and work were set aside, and though many of his works were copied religiously, it was his methods for attaining spiritual perfection, prophecy, and mystical experience which were emphasized and propagated. Modern scholarship has continued this long tradition of almost totally ignoring Abulafia's messianic claims and focusing on his Kabbalistic teachings, a process made easier by the adoption of the phenomenological approach.[8] Where Abulafia's messianic teachings have garnered attention, emphasis has been on the redemption of the individual as being the central axis of Abulafia's teaching, not the physical redemption of the Jews and the conclusion of the exile.[9]

Perhaps not surprisingly, Abulafia's messianic pretensions were embarrassing to his followers, particularly after 1291 when it became evident that he was not the Messiah, and probably also as a result of the sustained campaign and ban placed upon him by one of the leading rabbinic lights of the generation, Solomon ibn Adret. This might also explain why hardly any of Abulafia's overtly prophetic works have survived, and those that have can be interpreted in multifarious ways. This has allowed many Kabbalists over the centuries to ignore the messianic ramifications of Abulafia's teachings and concentrate on the techniques by which high levels of mystical experience and prophecy can be achieved. Yet Abulafia saw himself, first and foremost, as the expected Messiah who would bring the exile to a close, and his Kabbalistic teachings can only be fully appreciated if seen as part of that worldview. Internal redemption goes hand in hand with the external historical redemption that will bring humanity into true knowledge of God. Abulafia's reading of the biblical text is what informs his understanding of his times and mission, and is what allows him to receive the revelations that are the pivotal moments of his life. It is his claim to be the Messiah that gives him the authority to reveal the true meaning of the biblical text and the essence of Judaism. Hence, while Abulafia is primarily known as a Kabbalist, it is those teachings that inform his primary function as a messianic figure. Apocalyptic ideas are heavily dependent on a particular historical context, and Abulafia's messianism has to be understood in relation to the historical circumstances that conditioned him.[10] It is only by placing Abulafia within this historical context that much of what he wrote and preached begins to make sense. It is Abulafia himself who provides the clues that can help make sense of his life, and which show just how involved he was within his particular historical context, and how neither his teachings nor his activities can be divorced from the specific religious, intellectual, political, and geographic surroundings in which he flourished.

What causes someone to pronounce himself Messiah? Is it possible to identify the forces of history, or moments of catastrophe, that motivate individuals to swim against the current and take up the mantle of prophet or redeemer? In a fascinating discussion of the 'Isawiyya, a Jewish messianic movement in early Islam (ca. 755), Steven Wasserstrom enumerates the different stages in its development. First is the attempt at accommodation with the majority faith where the 'Isawiyya were able to appear to be true believers to Muslims, but also be accepted as Jews by their co-religionists. The second stage, the apocalyptic, was stirred by anti-Umayyad movements and a resurgence of hope that with the fall of the crumbling dynasty, the messianic era would start. According to both Muslim and Jewish sources, Abu 'Isa, the messianic figure, had an ascension experience, which led him to take on the mantle of Messiah.[11] This analysis shows the importance of the intimate ties between members of the minority and majority faith, and the significance of the broader historical picture in providing the context for the emergence of the Messiah figure. This may go some way in shedding light on what motivated Abraham Abulafia to pronounce himself Messiah.[12] In this case, however, it is the Christian surroundings that provided the context. The apocalyptic expectations among the Franciscans and others in Italy, coupled with age-old Jewish expectations for redemption and revelation, may shed light on Abulafia's psyche.[13]

There can be little doubt that 5000 AM, the start of the sixth millennium according to the Hebrew calendar, and Abulafia's birth in that portentous year would have been reason enough to jumpstart his messianic speculations. Yet, though aroused to go and find the Sambation River when he was twenty, an act with clear messianic undertones, he did not proclaim himself Messiah until 1276. By that time, Abulafia had traveled widely, and spent time in close proximity with Christians who were expecting major events to occur in the near future. Abulafia's adoption of 1290 as the year of redemption can only be understood in the broader historical context. As we shall see, Abulafia's apocalyptic calculations came from within his own tradition (though with some connection to the Christian Anno Domini), using accepted methods and authoritative texts. However, the importance of 1290, given that it was already fifty years into the sixth millennium can only be appreciated when seen in the Christian context.

The first chapter deals with that Christian context, introducing Joachim of Fiore and explaining some of the central concepts in his writings. Central tenets of Joachimism that resonate in Abulafia's writing are also set out. Joachim died in 1202, but his teachings were passed on via the order he established, the Florensians, the Cistercians, and the Franciscans. All these orders were instrumental in the copying of manuscripts of Joachim's works and in the composition of pseudo-Joachimite works that were to be of major importance in the late thirteenth century. The Franciscans play a pivotal role in this story, and their fascination with Joachim is also elaborated, as well as the teachings that would be so instrumental for their relationship with Abulafia.

A detailed biography of Abraham Abulafia is the subject of the second chapter. Unlike most other medieval mystical authors, Abulafia was relatively forthcoming with biographical details, though what is told is accidental and related to the purpose of the given work. However, looking at the broader historical context and using his works carefully, it is possible to piece together a reasonably detailed portrait of Abulafia's life, influences, motivations, ideas, and activities. It is also possible to see how his thought developed over some twenty years of creative activity. A picture emerges of a man who came to believe that he was the expected Messiah, that his mission was to prepare both Jews and Christians for the fast approaching end, and that he had been given the key to the true interpretation of the biblical text and knowledge of the Divine name.

The next chapter deals with Abulafia's views on universal salvation, a theme with great relevance to Joachim's teachings on the coming together of Gentiles and Jews in the third age. In contradistinction to many of his Christian and Jewish contemporaries who focused on the particularistic aspects of messianic times, Abulafia develops a theory of universal salvation based on a rather sophisticated understanding of history, political entities, and language. He suggests that the Divine economy planned for different religions and this leads him to posit a coming together of the nations of the world in a state of spiritual knowledge of the Divine name in a way very reminiscent of the Calabrian abbot. This implies that for Abulafia, contemporary Judaism was also in a transient phase, and though the closest to perfection, it would also be surpassed.

One particular historical event that has been the focus of some discussion is Abulafia's famous attempt to have a papal audience in August 1280. This episode has been analyzed from different perspectives with disagreement among scholars as to where he got the idea from and what exactly he intended to say to the pope. Much has been made of the sudden death of the pope on the very night before Abulafia intended to have his audience. However, the significance of the date he chose, and of this event in the broader historical context has not been examined. Hence, the penultimate chapter reexamines Abulafia's visit to Rome in 1280 in some detail. Abulafia's attitude toward Christianity is crucial for understanding what he intended to achieve from his papal audience. A close reading of the texts shows that the audience was to occur on a very precise day at a very auspicious moment, and the death of the pope on that very day, after his refusal to receive Abulafia, was a clear sign that he was the Messiah, that the power of Christianity was on the wane and that the end of days was fast approaching.

The previous chapters have established just how dependent Abulafia's messianic ideas were on his historical context and his appropriation of Joachimite concepts. The last chapter attempts to set out possible reasons why elements in the Franciscan order may have been interested in helping Abulafia see the pope. A Jew preaching the end of Christianity and other blasphemies would surely not have gained much sympathy from his Christian contemporaries, yet brief comments in Abulafia's works allow us to construct a network of people, both Jewish and Christian, that Abulafia, directly or indirectly, was in touch with who could have been in a position to help him arrange the audience. While these Christian and Jewish figures may have had different motivations for helping, or at least not hindering, Abulafia, and while not, in any way, conclusive, this chapter shows that there may have been some method to his madness.

The writing of this book was facilitated by the sudden appearance of reasonably good and reliable editions of almost all of Abulafia's extant works. Though found in hundreds of manuscripts, aside from the publication of a few short works and excerpts in the late nineteenth and twentieth century, nothing had been published.[14] This by no means reflected a lack of interest in Abulafia's Kabbalah, but was the direct result of the ban promulgated by Solomon ibn Adret against his works. This ban was so effective, that it was only toward the end of the last decade of the twentieth century, some six hundred years after the ban was placed, and some four hundred years after the invention of the printing press, that ultra-orthodox Jews in Jerusalem, students of Abulafian Kabbalah, decided to print his works. In order to do so, they had to find ways to circumvent the ban of a figure still considered within the orthodox world as a major Halachic authority. The editor of the series does this in the introduction to the first volume by showing that many other great rabbis over the generations had ignored the ban and studied Abulafia's works. The editor names and cites many of these sources to justify his project. His reasoning is that if those great luminaries over the ages could ignore the ban, then surely, it is permissible for him to do the same.[15]

Given that these editions are readily available, and that the purpose of this book is not to deal with the intricacies of Abulafian Kabbalah but to place Abulafia within the historical context in which he was active, I have cited from the printed editions. I have also compared the editions with the manuscripts and have found them to be of a high standard. Clearly, great care was taken when preparing the works for printing because Abulafia's Kabbalah is dependent on letter combinations and if these are not copied accurately, it is impossible to follow the teachings. Thus, there is a vested interest in good editions of the works, and where mistakes have been discovered new editions of that work have been made available. However, where serious discrepancies between the printed text and the manuscripts appear this has been pointed out.[16]

The timing of the appearance of these volumes is interesting in itself, the first volume, not Abulafia's first work, but definitely his most popular, judging by the number of extant manuscripts, *Hayei ha-Olam ha-Ba* (Life in the World to Come) appeared in July–August 1999 and the rest continued to appear over a three-year period.[17] From the introductions to the various volumes, what seems to be of paramount interest is Abulafia's Kabbalah itself and the secret teachings that lie therein, but there remains a nagging feeling that the printing of these works in Jerusalem at this juncture in time and in this historical-political context is not unconnected with Abulafia's contention that it was permissible to reveal and write down these secret teachings because the end is nigh.

Joachim and Joachimism in Italy

And once more the understanding of Scripture, or revelation, or the key of David, will be given to a person or multitude, and I think rather to a multitude.

—St. Bonaventure, *Collationes* 16:29

In his sermons on the six days of creation, St. Bonaventure identified Francis as the founder of the order of contemplatives that will flourish at the end of time. This followed his identification of Francis in the *Legenda maior,* the official biography of the saint, as "the angel of the sixth seal" of Revelation. The above citation is suggestive of the important role given to both the founder and the Franciscan order itself in the events leading up to the end of days; events which, according to Bonaventure, had already been set in motion.

It is not really known how and when elements in the Franciscan order became aware of the teachings of the Calabrian abbot Joachim of Fiore and their ramifications for that order. The incredible success and growth of the Franciscans was seen as a mixed blessing by some in the order who felt that the teachings of their founder had been set aside in the pursuit of glory and power. The simplicity, humility, poverty, and devotion of St. Francis had been trampled over in the larger context of papal politics and the needs of an all-powerful Church. Yet, the encounter with Joachim and his writings suddenly gave new meaning to the events of the past years, and seemed to give a central role to the Franciscans in the years leading up to the end of time. St. Francis became a harbinger of the end of time, the angel of the sixth seal, and his order, or at least those of the order who followed his teachings, represented one of the two orders of "spiritual men" leading others into a new age. Though for reasons self-evident, these ideas were not expressly set out in the writings of the Calabrian abbot, the central themes could be teased out of them, and they were given more impetus in works attributed to Joachim written in Italy in the coming decades.

Joachim of Fiore (ca. 1135–1202) elaborated his conception of history as progressing toward salvation in a number of works written mainly in the last decade of the twelfth century.[1] In his thirties, he had made a pilgrimage to the Holy Land and there, supposedly on Mount Tabor, had a vision, the first of three, that gave him a general understanding of the way he was to read the biblical text. However, it was with the gift of "spiritual intelligence," granted him in the other two visions at the Cistercian monastery of Casamari in 1184, that he realized that he possessed the key to interpreting the biblical texts that revealed the patterns of history and its progression toward the end of times. Though already engaged with the idea of concordance between the Old and New Testament in a work written prior to the visions in Casamari, it was those visions that provided him with the mature understanding present in his central works: the *Liber concordia Novi ac Veteris Testamenti, Expositio in Apocalypsim, Psalterium decem chordarum,* and the *Liber figurarum.*[2] Joachim developed patterns of twos and threes, the former based on the two Testaments, the latter on the three persons of the Trinity as they are understood to have been revealed in history.

Joachim's close reading of the Old Testament led him to see it as a key for understanding the events of the New Testament down to the current times. The methodology was one of concordance, which he explained as being a harmony that reflects similarity in character, but not in dignity between the two periods, meaning that the New Testament was more perfect than the Old. He envisioned the Testaments as two trees, the first growing from Adam and ending with the birth of Christ, the second starting from Uziah, king of Judah and ending with Christ's second coming. According to Joachim's detailed calculations, each tree contained sixty-three generations divided into three groups of twenty-one, though the generations on each tree differed in duration, the first being carnal, the second more spiritual. The Old Testament tree was divided as follows: from Adam to Isaac, and then forty-two generations from

Jacob to the first coming of Christ. The New Testament tree, with its trunk starting from King Uziah, the king of Judah and contemporary of the prophet Isaiah who, according to Joachim, started preaching the Gospel, also had three groups, two of which, implying forty-two generations were to pass from the coming of Christ until the onslaught of the Antichrist. The length of a New Testament generation was thirty years, because this represented the age of Christ when he started to have disciples, his spiritual children, implying that the coming of the antichrist would be in 1260 (forty-two generations of thirty years' duration each). The twelve tribes and the twelve churches (seven in Asia and the five metropolitan churches of Rome, Constantinople, Alexandria, Antioch, and Jerusalem) are the branches of the trees emerging from Jacob and Christ respectively.[3] In the same way that it was from the branch of the tribe of Judah that Christ emerged, so it will be from the branch of the Roman Church that the second coming will issue.[4]

But it was the book of *Revelation* that provided Joachim with the framework for understanding the internal structure of each of the trees, or the historical periods they represented. He understood the seven seals of the book (Revelation 5) to represent seven periods (*tempora*) of persecution of the Jews in the Old Testament, which, using the idea of concordance, implied that there would also be seven persecutions of the church. The Jews had been persecuted by the Egyptians, Canaanites, Syrians, Assyrians, Chaldeans, Medes, and Greeks, and the Christians by the Jews, by the pagans, by the Persians, Goths, Vandals, and Lombards simultaneously, by the Saracans, and now in his own day, by the German emperors. That left two more persecutions, with the last, represented by Antiochus in the Old Testament, being the Antichrist. However, the last two persecutions (the sixth and seventh seals) would have to happen concurrently as the second coming was close at hand.

The Trinitarian pattern of three was probably the outcome of the second of his visions at Casamari in 1184, and resulted in a significant departure from previous understanding of the apocalypse. St. Augustine had proposed that the thousand-year reign of the saints with Christ was the present time of the Church, and that therefore, all that was expected in the future was the second coming and final judgment.[5] Joachim's understanding was, however, that the millennium was yet to come and was a third period that would be ushered in after the defeat of the Antichrist. Thus, Joachim outlined the history of the world as one divided into three statuses, each one connected to one of the three persons of the Trinity, and reflecting the relationship within the Trinity. Because there is progression in history toward salvation, the first status, that of the Father, is one in which "men lived according to the flesh," the second, that of the Son, "in which men live between two poles, that is between the flesh and the spirit," and the future third status, that of the Holy Spirit, "in which people live according to the spirit."[6] Yet, the three statuses are interlinked in that the status of the Son, that of the current Church, has its roots in the status of the Father, with Aaron signifying priesthood and Isaiah evangelization. The third status has its roots in both the first and second status; Elijah or his disciple Elisha along with St. Benedict signifying the monastic spiritual way of life that will dominate in the third status.

Elijah is a pivotal figure in that he is the symbol of the Holy Spirit in both the first and third status. He is identified with fire in that he brought down the Divine fire on Mount Carmel when he confounded the prophets of Ba'al and he was taken up to heaven in a chariot of fire. He announces the procession of the Holy Spirit from the Father, and he will announce the procession of the Holy Spirit from the Son as the second status comes to an end. He is linked with Moses in that they both spoke with Jesus when he transfigured on Mount Tabor (the very mountain upon which Joachim's first vision supposedly took place),[7] and his connection with John the Baptist is also intimated in the Gospels in that the latter was the herald of Jesus' first coming.[8] Elijah is the perfect figure to illustrate the double pattern of twos and threes, or the historical and spiritual progressions that are completely interlinked in Joachim's thought. The pattern of twos or the historical is more traditional in that it presents history progressing from the time of the Old Testament to the New Testament, which will last till the end of time in the second coming. The Trinitarian pattern is innovative in that it places the third status within history, and posits a spiritual progression toward a more perfect state of being emerging from, but not replacing, the New Testament with its roots in the Old Testament as well.[9] Elijah represents that spiritual progression within history as he has a crucial role in illuminating the revelation of the Trinity in history; the procession of the Holy Spirit from both the Father and Son, and the initiation of the third status, which will be the fruition of both the first and second status.

Central for Joachim's understanding of the unfolding of Divine revelation in history was the Tetragrammaton (IEUE).[10] This is first worked out in Joachim's *Expositio in Apocalypsim* and also in the *Psalterium decem chordarum,* which was written as a result of the Easter vision in Casamari that clarified the meaning of the Trinity. In his reading of Revelation 1:8 in his commentary on the Apocalypse, Joachim shows how the Alpha and Omicron represent the Trinity and Unity. He does this using the Tetragrammaton which appears as a unity in the Omicron, and divided into IE at the apex of the Alpha, and EU and UE respectively at the bottom of the two uprights of the letter. For Joachim, this was proof that the Trinity had been revealed to the biblical Jews from within their most holy of Divine names.[11] Toward the end of the second book of the *Psalterium decem chordarum* Joachim writes: "Note the end of your questions [regarding the nature of the Trinity] in this holy name of God which is IEVE. IE is one name which refers to the Father, EV is one name which has reference to the Son, VE is one name which refers to the Holy Spirit. Indeed IEVE is one name, but it cannot simply be possible to refer to the Father alone or the Son alone or the Holy Spirit, but at the same time to all three. . . ." [12] The figure of the Psaltry with ten strings from the Oxford manuscript of the *Liber figurarum* has the Tetragrammaton in the central *rosa* (which represents the Omicron) with the inscription around it *Deus omnipotens, Sancta Trinitas unus Deus.*[13]

This is shown in greater detail in the Trinitarian figure of the *Liber figurarum* where the three central interlocking circles indicate both the passage of time from the Creation to the end of the world and the working of the persons of the Trinity in the three statuses.[14]

The figures of the Alpha and the cursive Omega, on the upper and lower right of the central circles indicate the relationship between the three persons. In the Alpha, the Father (IE) sends forth both the Son (EU) and Holy Spirit (UE) and they are one as the IEUE in the middle indicates. In the cursive Omega which represents the mission of the Trinity in history, the Holy Spirit (E) proceeds from both the Father (I) and the Son (U). This double procession is indicated in history, as can be seen beneath the Omega. Moses inaugurates the first status; Elijah announces the roots of the second status within the first. John the Baptist inaugurates the second status with Elijah again coming as herald for the third status. The Alpha and Omega come together in the three interlocking circles in that they meet in the middle of the first circle with the IEUE in the small circle indicating the oneness, and then the emergence into history with the Father (IE) in the first circle, the Son (EU) in the second, and the Holy Spirit (UE) in the third. The first circle is the time of the Old Testament, the second and third the New Testament, though the third circle represents the spiritual fulfillment of both the Testaments. Here the connection between the name *Adonai* and the Tetragrammaton is also explicitly spelled out, in that in the epicenter of the three circles the two are mentioned together (*Adonai, IEUE, Tetragrammaton*).[15]

According to Joachim, he was living in the fortieth generation of the second status, that of the Son, the New Testament, and the Church, or in the immediate period before the opening of the sixth seal followed by the seventh in the forty-first and forty-second generations. These generations would be signified by the persecutions of the sixth and seventh heads of the great beast of Revelation 12, with the latter head being the Antichrist.[16] These calculations pointed to the years 1200–1260 as the last two generations, though it was only in the *Liber figurarum* that he actually mentioned the year 1260.[17] Joachim predicted that in these generations, there would also appear two orders of *viri spirituales* (spiritual men) who would mediate and guide others toward the new age, one of these more contemplative, the other more active. He also speculated that in the sixth *tempora* of the second status, a pope

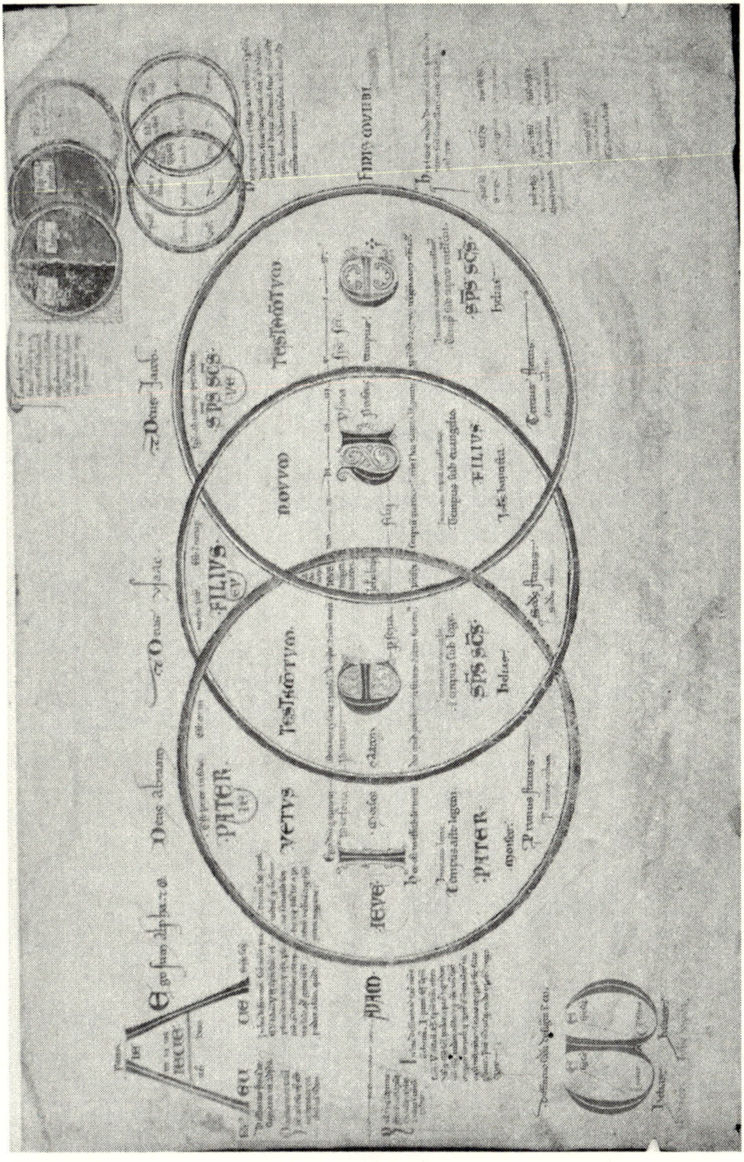

Figure 1.1 Trinitarian Figure with Tetragrammaton (IEVE). Taken from Joachim's *Liber figurarum,* Oxford, Corpus Christi College, Ms. 255A, f. 7v. *By permission of the President and Fellows of Corpus Christi College, Oxford.*

would come who would be sent from Babylon to Jerusalem to reform and renew the Church and who would face the Antichrist.[18]

Though it is immediately apparent that Joachim's works did not die with him, there was an interlude of some forty years before matters started to get out of hand. During this period, Joachim had taken a battering, in that the IV Lateran Council condemned his teachings on the Trinity while endorsing those of Peter Lombard.[19] However, in contrast, Gregory IX, in his bull of July 13, 1234 canonizing St. Dominic, referred to the order Joachim had established as one of the pillars of the Church.[20] Additionally, there are a few citations of some of Joachim's works by theologians in Paris in the 1230s, but, in general, his impact seems to have been minimal. However, by the 1240s matters had changed considerably.

It is important to remember that Joachim lived and wrote in southern Italy and Sicily, and the available evidence, though not extensive, indicates that these places were important centers of Joachimism in the second half of the thirteenth century. The copies of Joachim's genuine works as well as the pseudo-Joachim biblical commentaries and various compilations of prophecies and collections of figures were all seemingly products of the South, whether they were carried out or redacted by Florensians, Cistercians, or Franciscans.[21] One of these, the pseudo-Joachimite commentary on Jeremiah, may be based on an original work by Joachim, but was substantially redacted and adapted by either Florensians or Cistercians, and then Franciscans in Calabria.[22] The work reflects disillusionment with elements within the Cistercian Order who had supported the condemnation of Joachim's treatise on the Trinity in 1215, but also emphasizes the important role of the order in the monastic society of the third status. The redaction of the original work, probably composed ca. 1244, is far more explicit than Joachim's real works in looking forward to 1260, identifying the forces of the Antichrist, and in giving a central role to the mendicant orders leading in to the third status. It also reflects the current political situation, in particular the ongoing controversy between emperor and papacy, with the former, the formidable Frederick II, being identified with the sixth or seventh head of the great beast of

Revelation.[23] The geographical sequences, which concentrate on the dioceses of Italy and Sicily in the *Pseudo-Isaiah* written between 1260–1266 by Franciscans, the identification of Frederick II as the seventh head of the beast in the *Praemissiones,* and the recalculation of the date of the start of the third status to 1290 in the latter and in a collection of Joachim's works and figures also point at southern Italy as being central to how Joachim's works were understood and applied.[24] One of the best witnesses to thirteenth-century Joachimism, Salimbene de Adam, a Franciscan chronicler of great import originally from Parma, also provides much substantiating evidence in that many of the Joachimites mentioned in his chronicle come from Sicily and southern Italy.

While it is unclear where and when the Franciscans became aware of Joachim's writings, and how they came to identify themselves as one of the two orders predicted by Joachim, and their founder as the angel of the sixth seal, by the 1240s these ideas were well established. In 1255 in a joint encyclical, Humbert de Romanis and John of Parma, generals of the Dominicans and Franciscans, viewed their orders as those sent to save the world, using Joachite imagery to substantiate this fact.[25] St. Bonaventure, in his *Legenda maiora,* which was adopted by the order in 1266 as the only official life of Francis, referred to the latter as having come in the spirit and power of Elijah and to being the sixth angel of the Apocalypse.[26] Much of the Franciscan interest in Joachim is doubtlessly due to the controversies that broke out immediately after Francis's death about the legitimacy and binding authority of his Last Testament and the issue of poverty and property. Those who tried to uphold the Last Testament and live to a severe standard of evangelical poverty set out by Francis found themselves increasingly on the defensive. They may have taken courage from Joachim's teachings which let them see Francis, as was Christ before him, as the initiator, and themselves as forerunners of the new age.

It is Frederick II's advance northward over the Alps in late 1239 that provides direct evidence of Franciscan interest in Joachim.[27] Salimbene de Adam reports that while he was in Pisa, a Florensian abbot, afraid that the emperor would ransack his monastery fled there bringing with him all the works of Joachim that he had. This abbot was Salimbene's first teacher in Joachite matters and, as a result, Rudolph of Saxony, a Franciscan lector at Pisa, gave up his study of theology and became a great Joachimite.[28] Salimbene goes on to name many others in the order with whom he was in contact who adopted Joachim's teachings, among them, John of Parma who would become minister general of the order in 1247, Hugh of Digne, Bartholemew Guiscolus, and Gerard of Borgo San Donnino who would stir up a hornet's nest in Paris. The latter two probably became Joachimites in Sicily, and Bartholemew had been a guardian of the Franciscan convent in Capua.[29] Hugh of Digne was based at Hyères in Provence, and as Salimbene reports, was a great Joachimite and close colleague of John of Parma and a magnet for many others in the order interested in the Calabrian abbot's teachings. Thus, it is, from the late 1230s onward, most likely in Sicily, Calabria, and Naples where Joachim's teachings were well established, that they took root in the Franciscan order. Hence, Salimbene's chronicle, though mostly written with hindsight between 1283–1287, is crucial for showing the extent of the network of Franciscans who had adopted and adapted Joachite ideas.[30]

Salimbene describes the traumatic events surrounding the publication in Paris of Gerard's *Introductorius in evangelium eternum* in 1254, which also has to be seen in light of the opposition to the mendicants from many elements in the Church. Monks should be in monasteries, and not wandering around parishes preaching and undermining the role of the local priests and clerics. The presence of the mendicants in the universities was also a source of great controversy as they competed with the secular canons for the chairs of theology. Their supposed adherence to absolute poverty also made them targets for those who saw them as a dangerous innovation in the Church. Developments and disagreements within the order regarding issues as central as the interpretation of the extent of poverty, particularly in relation to the use of property, strict observance of the rule and the legal standing of the Last Testament, the importance of learning, and the whole question of

Francis's intentions were also putting considerable strain on the order.[31] Facing this external and internal opposition, there was comfort to be found for those in the Franciscan order who adopted Joachim's teachings, because he seemed to have predicted the arrival at the end of the second status of two monastic orders who would roam the world spreading light rather than being cloistered.

Clearly, Gerard of Borgo San Donnino wrote with the fast-approaching date of 1260 in mind, and his understanding of Joachim's teachings led him to believe that if each previous status had its own gospel, then it stood to reason that in the progression toward the age of the Holy Spirit, a new gospel would be revealed.[32] According to the commission that examined Gerard's work, it included some of Joachim's major works with an introduction that suggested, among other things, that the New Testament would be superseded in the same way the Old was, and that the *Eternal Gospel* was identical with Joachim's teachings.

The publication of the *Eternal Gospel,* which would have been considered in bad taste at any time, was only grist for the mill to those seeking to challenge and discredit the Franciscans in the highest circles. Gerard was an anomaly, who was rapidly dispatched back to Capua in 1256, and his claims were not widely accepted, but this scandal drew the attention of many to the influence of Joachim and writings attributed to him on the order.[33] William of St. Amour, the chief advocate of the seculars against the encroachment of the mendicants at the university in Paris reported that Joachim's teachings had powerful admirers in Rome, and not only among the Franciscans.[34] This claim is substantiated by Salimbene who mentions that the Roman senator in 1257–1258, Lord Brancaleone of Bologna, had a copy of Gerard's book, and clearly other copies were making the circuit.[35] Angelo of Clareno, one of the leaders of the spirituals in the fourteenth century, implies that there were many who were attracted to the teachings of Joachim, and although the important landmark of 1260 passed without anything happening, disillusionment did not imply abandonment of Joachite teachings. After 1260, there appeared in southern Italy Joachimite recalculations of the forty-two generations that began at the start of

Christ's ministry rather than from the nativity. That implied that the new age would start in 1290.[36]

Salimbene provides interesting instances of reinterpretation of Joachim's teachings, and shows how widespread these ideas were in certain circles. Though Salimbene writes that Joachim never set out a date for the coming of the Antichrist and the end of history, the commentary on Jeremiah talks specifically about 1260, and in 1248 or thereabouts, Salimbene seems to accept this relying on his study of the text with two other Joachimite brothers, one from Capua and the other from Sicily.[37] However, the chronicle seems to indicate that at a certain moment Salimbene became a little more circumspect about Joachimism. This is based on a passage wherein a Brother Bartholomew of Mantua who had been a minister in Rome and Milan took Salimbene to task for having adhered to the teachings of Joachim, and the latter comments that since the death of Frederick II (the recorded discussion between Hugh of Digne and the Dominican Peter must have taken place before this as it is one of the central issues in their disputation over matters Joachite) in 1250 and the passing of 1260 he had laid these teachings aside and, "now I plan to believe in nothing save what I can see."[38] However, this remark was made in the aftermath of the controversy surrounding John of Parma who had been forced to resign, to a senior member of the order who was clearly not enamored either by John or by his Joachite leanings. Salimbene's remark clearly has to be seen as politically expedient at that moment in time, and should not be taken too seriously.[39] The chronicle, written in the 1280s is suffused with Joachimite ideas and indeed, after this discussion with Bartholomew, Salimbene is full of praises for Joachim and his writings, and his understanding of the place of the Franciscans in the coming dispensation remains unchanged. Indeed, when writing about 1260, Salimbene sees in the flagellant movement the start of the fulfilment of the Joachite prophecy, and for instance, in 1284, Salimbene mentions studying a commentary on the Apocalypse by a Brother Bertold of Germany adding, "And I did this in order to know the meanings of those angels, but I was not interested in the rest because I had the exposition of Joachim which I consider to be the best of all the others."[40] Salimbene again cites the pseudo-Jeremiah commentary in 1287, where Joachim supposedly gives the Franciscans a prominent role in the times leading toward the third status.[41]

Following 1260, and notwithstanding the appearance of the flagellants, Salimbene seems to have been aware of the attempt to recalculate and date the start of the third status to 1290. Though he never mentions this specific year, Salimbene seems to be prepared to accept that the generation between 1260 and 1290 is the crucial one in the buildup to Joachim's third status. Referring to the year 1278, while discussing why the Holy Sepulchre had not been recaptured from the Muslims even though numerous crusades had been planned, Salimbene cites from Luke 21:24 ("And Jerusalem shall be trodden down by the gentiles, till the times of the nations be fulfilled") and Revelation 11:2 ("But the court, which is without the temple, cast out, and measure it not: because it is given unto the gentiles, and they shall tread the holy city under foot forty-two months"). Basing himself on the pseudo-Jeremiah commentary, Salimbene explains that the forty-two months represent the forty-two generations from Christ to the year 1260, when the flagellants appeared on the scene. Yet he adds, that each generation is of thirty years duration because Jesus was baptized by John at that age. Salimbene cites Revelation 11:3 ("I will give unto my two witnesses, and they shall prophesy a thousand two hundred and sixty days clothed in sackcloth") to indicate the significance of that number and shows that days should be read as years. In his genuine works, Joachim refers to the length of the New Testament generations as being thirty years so there is nothing new here. However, Salimbene's comment is in line with other post-1260 southern Italian traditions which calculate the generations starting from the passion (or baptism), rather than the nativity and hence, arrive at a date of 1290 for the start of the third status.[42] Salimbene states that it is Divine will that the Holy Sepulchre has not been recaptured and that there has not been any emperor after Frederick II.[43] Yet, the juxtaposition of this discussion with the Joachite calculation of the forty-two generations seemingly implies that events that started in 1260 will come to a conclusion in the following generation. This reading is supported by Salimbene's reference to the Council of Lyon in 1274 where the Greeks supposedly returned to the fold, and the following paragraphs deal with the upcoming conversion of the Jews and Gentiles based on Joachim's understanding of these events.[44]

According to Joachim's view of salvation, there is a progression from original sin, throughout history toward the third status, and this also points toward a return to the pristine spiritual state before the Fall. In other words, over time, there is a movement away from carnality and worldly affairs toward spiritual life and true knowledge of God. Joachim believed that if the first status was that of the Old Testament and the second of the New Testament, the third, which is intertwined with the two proceeding ones, will be a true and spiritual understanding of both Testaments. Spiritual intelligence is also refined as the third status approaches and will produce spiritual men who will live in this true knowledge. In a fascinating reading of the biblical story of Jacob, this also implied a union of Christians and Jews in the third status. Jacob's leaving of the Land of Israel signifies his move from the first to the second status where he becomes blessed with children and wealth. His conflict with Laban and his sons who were jealous of Jacob's success represents the conflict between the contemplatives of the Church and the clergy. Jacob's return to the land of his forefathers signifies the return to the Jews. Citing Paul: "When the fullness of the gentiles comes in, so all Israel shall be saved" (Romans 11:25–26), Joachim understood this to mean that when the perfected Christians returned to the Land, they and the Jews would be as one: "indeed, when Jacob completes his itinerary, he comes to his father, for at the end of the sixth time of the sixth age . . . there is a union of the gentile and the Hebrew people, and there will be one fold and one shepherd."[45] In contradistinction to his predecessors and contemporaries for whom the conversion of the Jews was a central element of the end of days, Joachim envisioned a union of Shem and Yefet, of Jew and Christian in the third status in knowledge of God and in a spiritual state.[46]

The time of the return of the Jews to the fold and the union of the two nations was to occur at the end of the second status as the spiritual perfection of Christianity was to become apparent. Robert Lerner's study has shown that Joachim's teachings about the Jews resonated among the Franciscans who adopted his teachings. The redactors of the Jeremiah and Isaiah commentaries were aware of this concept and other central figures such as Hugh of Digne, though not mentioning it expressly, seem to have accepted it.[47] Hugh asked Salimbene to make a copy of Joachim's *Treatise on the Four Gospels* for John of Parma and in that work Joachim's hopes for the imminent return of the Jews are most prominent.[48] Interestingly, Salimbene himself comments with respect to the conversion of the Jews: "See Joachim's book, for it is a most beautiful and delightful commentary filled with truth," seemingly referring to the aforementioned treatise.[49] In addition, Gerard of Borgo San Donnino also seems to have included some of these ideas in his introduction to the *Eternal Gospel* or in his glosses to the text of Joachim's *Liber concordia*. Salimbene's chronicle shows the intimate connections between Joachimites in the Franciscan Order, the discussions that were held and the books that were copied and studied. Thus, this notion of a spiritual union between Christian's and Jews seems to have had a large number of adherents in southern Italy and probably Sicily as well.[50]

The establishment of the monastery of Fiore in the Sila Mountains in Calabria by Joachim also takes on apocalyptic tones. In a biography written by a Florensian almost immediately after Joachim's death, Fiore is described as the new Nazareth, from where the seed of the new Israel will spread forth.[51] Joachim saw his monastery as the locus of the new flowering of the spirit and it is for this reason that he named it Fiore, Flor, Flower, believing it to be the meaning of the Hebrew word *Nazeret* (Nazareth) as well.[52] The biography also depicts Joachim as a prophet of the exile and the restorer of Israel, using imagery found in Jeremiah and Ezekiel, ideas found in Joachim's own works as well. Joachim suggests that the third temple and city of Jerusalem will be rebuilt by the modern exiles in the same manner that the second temple was built by the sons of the exiles from Judah. Yet, according to the biography and other pseudo-Joachimite texts, Joachim does not seem to be referring to the earthly Jerusalem and temple, but to Fiore, and southern Italy as the place where the new Jerusalem will flourish.[53] Joachim, the prophet of exile and redemption, predicts the fall of the earthly Jerusalem to the Muslims and sows the seed of redemption in the spiritual Holy Land to be found in southern Italy.[54]

Toward the end of the fourth book of the *Liber concordia,* Joachim talks about the new leader from Babylon, a universal pontifex of the New Jerusalem, who would arise in the forty-second generation and renew the teachings of the Christian faith and would preach the word of God.[55] For the Franciscans, the generation after 1260 was the forty-second generation and it seems clear that they were expecting this new leader to appear. Interestingly, in a conversation with the Cistercian abbot Adam of Persigny, in 1198, Joachim talked about the appearance of the Antichrist in Rome, which for him was the mystical Babylon. Joachim then went on to predict that Pope Innocent III would not have a successor, and that he himself might live to see the Antichrist. Thus, the idea was mooted that the Antichrist would appear in Rome and that there would be no successor to the pope, though eventually a new leader would arrive to lead the Church into the third status.[56] As shall be shown, Abulafia's appearance in Rome, his reference to himself as the Antichrist, and his message about the end of Christianity may have resonated in certain circles with teachings associated directly with Joachim regarding the tribulations of the church leading up to the third status.

As the following chapters will indicate, Abulafia clearly latched on to these teachings, and adopted and adapted them to reflect his worldview and understanding of the unfolding of events leading up to the end of times. It is most likely these Franciscans, whom he encountered during his perambulations around Sicily and southern Italy, who provided him with insights with which to interpret his own visions. Yet there are also grounds to consider the possibility that the Franciscan Joachimites might have found interest in Abulafia and they might have been prepared to entertain his ideas. This

Figure 1.2 The Trinitarian Tree Circles. The Jews and Gentiles merge in full bloom in the third status. Taken from Joachim's *Liber figurarum,* Oxford, Corpus Christi College, Ms. 255A. f. 12v. *By permission of the President and Fellows of Corpus Christi College, Oxford.*

is not to say that they accepted his interpretations and understanding of the biblical text, his messianic claims, or his predictions regarding upcoming events. More likely, they would have read him into the Joachimite texts that predicted the events leading up and into the third status.

In the *Praemissiones,* which presents adaptations and, sometimes, misrepresentations of Joachim's figures and is associated with the pseudo-Isaiah commentary, the figure of the seven seals indicates that the last tribulations or opening of the sixth and seventh seals would take place in *Soldanorum provincia* and *Italia.*[57] This also supports other indications in the revised figures, such as the seventh head of the dragon that connects the Hohenstaufen with Antichrist. Thus, Italy was to be the place where the final crises before the third status would begin. Joachim's portrayal of southern Italy as a place of spiritual renewal would also find resonance with Abulafia, who saw Sicily as the place of the renewal of prophecy and messianic revelation. There was also the idea that disaster was about to strike the papacy in the lead up to the transition to the third status, and Abulafia's mission to the pope might have been seen in that light.[58] In addition, Abulafia was preaching knowledge of the Tetragrammaton as the true essence of God, which for the Joachimites was the most sublime representation of the oneness and Trinitarian nature of God. As Salimbene indicates, the *Liber figurarum* was read frequently and one of the central figures, the three intertwined circles along with the Alpha, cursive Omega, and Omicron, is clear indication of the centrality of the Tetragrammaton.[59] Abulafia's calculation of 1290 as the year of redemption would also have struck chords with Joachimites in general as can be seen from the commentary on Isaiah and the collection of works found in the late-thirteenth-century manuscripts that recalculate the generations to 1290. And Abulafia's vision of history following the redemption in 1290, while not entirely palatable to the Joachimites in that, naturally, neither Christ nor Christianity play any part, would nevertheless have been of interest in that it portrayed a progression to a spiritual level of being, knowledge, and belief.

A Life Reviewed

Abraham Abulafia was born in interesting times. The territories of the Crown of Aragon, under the Count-King James I, the Conqueror, were rapidly expanding as the reconquest of the Iberian peninsula from the Muslims proceeded apace. Just a few years before he was born, in 1229, Majorca was retaken, and there was an ongoing campaign to capture Valencia. This was a period of formation, opportunity, and change as large new expanses of land needed to be settled and administrated.[1] For the Jews of the Crown, these were relatively peaceful and prosperous times. They were protected by the monarchy and were able to pursue their communal life and religious practice with little external interference.[2] There were, however, signs that this was not to last, as the Church, with growing confidence in its spiritual and temporal powers, along with its new mendicant orders, sought to impose its worldview on the secular rulers of Europe in all areas of life.

The Jewish communities did not exist in a vacuum and were troubled by many of the issues also vexing their Christian counterparts. From the late twelfth century, one of the most significant issues was the penetration of Greek philosophy, via the mediation and interpretation of the Muslims, into the ambit of both the Christians and Jews of western Europe. The availability of the works of Aristotle and his Arabic commentators, along with works dealing with astrology, astronomy, medicine, magic, among others, was starting to have a tremendous impact on thinkers of both religious denominations. For the Jews in Europe, this came to a head with the arrival and translation of Maimonides' works in the early thirteenth century, which caused an immense upheaval that lasted for more than a century. Maimonides' works were only the spark that ignited the fire, and the continuing controversy over the coming decades had less to do with his works per se.[3] His reputation as a great Halachic authority and leader eventually defused the criticism of his philosophical works. More crucial, however, as in the Christian world, was the issue of the study of philosophy in general and its use for the examination of matters of faith and the authoritative texts.

Coupled and intimately connected with this controversy was the appearance on the historical stage of what is commonly known as Kabbalah. Presented in the guise of a conservative reaction to the radical ideas of the philosophers and their adherents, but, in reality, radical in its own right, Kabbalah sought to redress the imbalance created by philosophical teachings in Jewish praxis. Though it is difficult to pinpoint the moment or trace the exact trajectory of its exponential growth, by the 1230s Kabbalah had a significant presence in the Jewish communities of the Crown and beyond, and there is documented evidence of major disagreements between the different schools. Though based on esoteric mystical speculation about the nature of the Godhead, Kabbalah had a practical and more public side in that it presented compelling reasons for the strict observance of the Commandments and gave meaning to the current state of the Jews in exile. These were important considerations in a turbulent and changing environment.[4]

By the time Abulafia was born, and indeed almost to the end of the 1260s, the unchallenged leader of the Jewish community was Nahmanides (Moshe ben Nahman). Though living in Gerona, he represented the community on various occasions including the Barcelona disputation of 1263. He was considered a Halachic authority and a learned man, and his strong personality was very influential in defusing the controversy and tensions that had arisen over the study of philosophy and the works of Maimonides and in determining the latter's orthodoxy. However, his worldview was that of a Kabbalist and his writings reflect that, though he was careful to conceal matters that he considered esoteric and suitable only for oral transmission. Thus, the religious and intellectual leadership of the time reflected the diversity of interests within the broader community, and the relations of that community with its Christian and (to a certain extent) Muslim surroundings.[5]

For the details of Abulafia's life, we are almost totally reliant on the quite impressive amount of biographical evidence that he provides in his literary corpus. The time and place of writing (not always supplied), along with other incidental facts mentioned in passing, the way his works develop over the years and the manner in which the material is presented, allow us to construct a portrait of his life and activities. Even at first glance, his life was a pretty remarkable one—there have not been many Jews who became convinced that they were the Messiah and who tried to have an audience with the pope, though Abulafia was something of a trend setter for the handful of Jews who followed in his footsteps.[6] Yet, when Abulafia's works are examined more closely, a lot more information about his life and intellectual development comes to light. Indeed, close analysis of his writing reveals a man who, though very certain about the imminent arrival of the final redemption, was able to continually redefine his own role in the drama leading up to the end of times.

Abulafia's life can be roughly divided into five periods. The first covers the early years of his life, till, at the age of twenty, he left Catalonia for the Holy Land. The second period is essentially one of study and intellectual growth leading up to the vision of late 1270. The third is a relatively short, but intense period of engagement with what is now referred to as ecstatic Kabbalah, lasting until another revelation in December 1276, which caused Abulafia to believe that he was the expected Messiah. The following nine years are full of messianic activity, including his visit to Rome, and come to a close in late 1285, when as a result of sudden enlightenment, Abulafia examines his life anew. While the apocalyptic expectations remain in this last period, his overtly messianic activity is tempered, and though he still sees himself as Messiah, he now appears to think that he will only be revealed in his full glory in 1290 or early 1291. The writings of this period put more emphasis on the way to achieve prophecy and personal salvation, and are less explicit about his messianic claims, though these are not absent.[7]

Abraham Abulafia was born in Saragossa probably in late 1239, after the start of the Jewish New Year (Sept. 1).[8] Shortly thereafter, the family moved to Tudela, where he grew up and studied Torah with his father. These were clearly formative years, as decades later Abulafia made reference to what his father taught him: "Bible with commentaries and grammar, in other words, all the Holy Scriptures, which is made up of twenty-four books. And I also studied with him some Mishna and Talmud, as he was my teacher in most matters."[9] Thus, Abulafia's grounding in the basic corpus of Jewish texts, biblical and postbiblical, was acquired during these years. Two more years were spent in Tudela after Abulafia's father died when he was eighteen, though he gives no details as to what he was doing.

Late 1239–1240, the year of Abulafia's birth, corresponds in the Hebrew calendar to the year 5000, the start of the sixth millennium, without doubt a momentous year in Jewish apocalyptic thinking.[10] Abulafia was very aware of the special significance of the year of his birth, as he believed that the start of the millennium signaled the return of prophetic revelation, and therefore, in the context of his later activities, the year of his birth was no coincidence. At the age of twenty in 1260, he wrote with hindsight, "The spirit of the Lord woke and shook me, and I left home and went straight to the Land of Israel by sea and land. And my purpose was to go to the Sambation River, but I could not get further than Acre because of the conflict between Ishmael and Esau."[11] Whether or not Abulafia was aware of the Joachite expectations for that year when he set out to find the mythical river, the passage, written some twenty-five years later, after a considerable amount of contact with propagators of Joachim's teachings, clearly sets this journey in an apocalyptic setting. The legends about the ten tribes exiled beyond the river and their ingathering at the time of the coming of the Messiah was well known.[12] The fact that Abulafia was awoken by the spirit of the Lord, presumably in order to discover whether the ingathering of the ten tribes had already begun, at a time of heightened expectation for some Christians in his immediate vicinity, points to his awareness, at least with hindsight, of the broader context.[13]

This voyage, which was curtailed because of the battle of En Jalut between the Mamluks and Mongols in 1260, marked the start of an intensive period of study in Greece and Italy. Abulafia's exact itinerary is unclear and it seems that he moved around a great deal, together with his wife whom he married either on the way out to the Holy Land or on his return.[14] However, it is clear that this was a formative period, in that he discovered philosophy and particularly metaphysics, first studying some of the works of Aristotle and then, more crucially, Maimonides' *Guide for the Perplexed*.[15]

In *Otzar Eden Ganuz* he wrote about this period:

> And the spirit of the Lord awakened me, and I took my wife and went to the waters of Ravenna to study Torah. And when I was in Capua, a town five days from Rome, I found a man named Rabbi Hillel, may his memory be blessed, an honourable, wise, intelligent philosopher and expert doctor, and I found him pleasing, and I studied with him a little philosophy and immediately was attracted to it, and made great effort to acquire knowledge of it, and I studied it day and night, and I was not satisfied until I had studied *The Guide for the Perplexed* many times over, and I afterwards taught it in many places.[16]

Abulafia spent some time in Ravenna before moving on to Capua probably after 1262.[17] The rabbi who became his teacher is Hillel of Verona, an interesting character in his own right, who, as Abulafia states, was a highly respected doctor and philosopher. Hillel had studied the writings of Maimonides with Rabbi Jonah Gerondi in Barcelona for a period of three years, which is of interest as Abulafia made his way to Barcelona after studying with Hillel. He was very involved in the Maimonidean controversy and intended, as he wrote in a letter, to try and organize a rabbinic conference in Syria where Maimonides' writings would, once and for all, be cleared of all heretical connotations. Hillel wrote a number of treatises and was also a friend of Maestro Gaio, a Jew who was physician to cardinals and possibly a pope, and he was acquainted with other philosophers in Rome such as Zerahiah ben Shaltiel Hen of Barcelona.[18] Hillel had a major disagreement with the latter over the interpretation of the *Guide,* with Zerahiah accusing him of attributing to Maimonides the use of Gematria. This is reminiscent of the use Abulafia was to make of the *Guide* and may be an indication of where some of his ideas stemmed from, though there is a possibility that Hillel took these ideas from Abulafia during later encounters between the two. Abulafia probably remained in contact with Hillel after a period of being his disciple, and it is possible that the latter was to some extent involved in Abulafia's attempt to meet with the pope.[19] The *Guide for the Perplexed* became increasingly more important for Abulafia and he eventually wrote three commentaries on the work revealing what he believed to be the thirty-six secrets hidden within it.[20]

Sometime in the 1260s, Abulafia returned to Catalonia and settled in Barcelona, a move that was to prove to be of great significance for his development. The city had a large and vibrant Jewish community still under the influence of Nahmanides and then his disciple Solomon ibn Adret who replaced him when he was forced to leave for the Holy Land in 1267. Being a port, Barcelona had always been an important center for the transmission of knowledge as ships coming from Alexandria, Sicily, Genoa, and other places doubtlessly carried ideas from far off places as well as cargo for trade.[21] Translations into Hebrew of works influenced by Sufism were carried out by scholars from this city, and these ideas clearly permeated the writings of Kabbalists whose works were influential on Abulafia. He himself mentions studying Bahya ibn Pakuda's *Book of the Duties of the Heart,* which is suffused with Sufi concepts and ideas.[22] It is also probable that during this period, Abulafia became familiar with the writings of the most famous Sufi to emerge from Andalusia, Ibn al-'Arabi. The presence of Islam in the Iberian Peninsula, and the close proximity between the adherents of the different faiths, raises the intriguing possibility that some of Abulafia's teachings may have had their roots in Isma'ili theology and Sufism. Central themes in the writings of Ibn al-'Arabi, particularly in the last great work he composed while in Andalusia, the *Book of the Fabulous Gryphon,* deal with the seal of sainthood, the perfection of man, and the acquisition of knowledge and prophecy.

All these concepts would play a major role in Abulafia's writing and in the way he perceived and presented himself and his mission.[23]

Though his writings suggest that it was only after a vision in late 1270 that Abulafia started studying *Sefer Yetzirah,* which was to be so central to his own Kabbalistic system, it seems that he was studying this work along with some of its commentaries prior to this. It is likely that in Barcelona he studied with Baruch Togarmi, who, as his name indicates, was probably of Turkish origin, and who wrote a commentary on *Sefer Yetzirah.*[24] Twice in his works Abulafia lists twelve commentaries that he had studied, some of a more philosophical, rather than mystical nature, and though he considered the philosophical expositions of the work to be less interesting and complete, they were still worthy of being studied.[25] On the list is the commentary written by Ezra of Gerona, whose mystical outlook is influenced by Sufi ideas and practices, and though his work is suffused with the theosophical structure of the Sefirot, which was not central to Abulafia's teachings, it clearly influenced him. Indeed, when Ezra's commentary is set side by side with Baruch Togarmi's, which deals with the combination of letters, some of the sources for Abulafia's teachings become immediately apparent.[26] Important also to Abulafia's development were the works of the Ashkenazi pietists which were well known in Barcelona and farther west in Castile as well. In addition, Abulafia lists a whole series of mystical-magical works that he had studied including the *Sefer ha-Bahir,* one of the foundational texts of thirteenth-century Kabbalah, and *Sefer Raziel,* a book with magical connotations.[27]

Indeed, after 1270 Abulafia was already developing his own and unique brand of Kabbalah, but from his works it is clear that he considered necessary a good grounding in both philosophy and theosophical Kabbalah. In a letter written after 1285 to Judah Salmon in Barcelona to defend himself from his detractors, it becomes apparent that Abulafia had been studying Kabbalah during the 1260s, and the visionary experiences at the start of the 1270s were the beginning of his prophetic awakening, and did not appear in a vacuum. He regards sefirotic Kabbalah as a necessary stage on the way to prophetic revelation of the Divine names, which he sees as a much superior knowledge, and he emphasizes that he had studied the former before being granted prophetic awakening.[28] Thus, before the vision in late 1270, which he saw as the start of his prophetic career, he would have had to have achieved a solid grounding in philosophy and theosophical Kabbalah.

Late in the year 1270, Abulafia had the prophetic vision that signaled the start of a fifteen-year period of many trials and tribulations, but also intense messianic activity.[29] Very important in this context is a biographical passage found toward the end of *Otzar Eden Ganuz,* a book divided into thirty-two chapters written in late 1285.[30] The purpose of the work, referred to briefly in the introduction, is to demonstrate that Abulafia was truly a wise man (he refers to himself as a shepherd based on Jeremiah 3:15) qualified to reveal the ultimate truth, which is not known to those who consider themselves to be the wise men of the generation.[31] This ultimate truth is the secret of the Divine names by which one can be elevated to the level of prophet and attach oneself to the Active Intellect. Regarding this period, Abulafia writes:

> And when I was *aleph lamed* [thirty-one] years old in Barcelona, I was awakened by God from my sleep, and I studied *Sefer Yetzira* with its commentaries, and the hand of God was upon me. And I wrote books of wisdom based upon them, and wonderful books of prophecy, and my soul was alive within, and the spirit of the Lord moved my heart, and the spirit of holiness was raised in me. And I saw wonderful and terrible visions, by means of wonders and signs, and in general, there were about me spirits of zealousness. And I saw visions and phantasms, and I was tormented, for I found no-one who could guide me along the path. And therefore, I was like a blind man for *tet-vav* [fifteen] years, and Satan bedeviled me. And I was driven for *yud-heh* [fifteen] years by the visions I saw to fulfill the words of the Torah and bring the second curse to a conclusion, until God granted me some knowledge/foresight (*m'ada*). And God was with me as my aid from the year *aleph-lamed* [thirty-one] till the year *mem-heh* [forty-five] to guard me from any trouble. And at the start of the year *aleph-lamed-yud-heh* [Eliah, forty-six] the prophet, God desired me and brought me into the Divine sanctuary. And it

> is at this moment that I have completed this book which I wrote here in Messina for my dear disciple, distinguished, pleasing, intelligent, understanding, desiring to know the truth of the pure Torah, the first of the aforementioned seven, R. Saadiah.

Abulafia's choice of letters from the Hebrew alphabet with their numerical value to denote a particular year and the period is significant because, for him, the letters are the most important tool of reference for reaching the truth, for knowing God and creation. Hence, the letter notations Abulafia chooses give an indication of how he perceived himself in relation to God within this particular time period. The year when Abulafia had his second awakening in Barcelona, *aleph-lamed,* has the numerical value of thirty-one and spells one of the (lesser) names of God—*El* and the current year, *aleph-lamed-yud-heh* with a numerical value of forty-six, also spells Eliah whom Abulafia identifies, as the following words indicate, with Elijah the Prophet.[32] Abulafia clearly views himself, at this later period in time, as can be seen elsewhere in his works, as or like Elijah, as a messenger elected by God, to be the harbinger of redemption. At that moment, in Messina in late 1285, Abulafia had finally achieved the highest prophetic level and entered the Holy of Holies.[33]

In the middle of the passage, Abulafia describes this fifteen-year period from the revelation in Barcelona to the current year in two opposing ways, using different letter notations. The first description using the letters *tet-vav* is connected with Satan and blindness, and the second using the letters *yud-heh,* the first two letters of the Tetragrammaton, is connected with visions and Divine aid. Sometimes, Abulafia describes Satan as the thing in creation farthest away from true being, but more generally in his writing, Satan refers to the imagination (*dimyon*).[34] In addition, the letters *yud* and *heh,* the first two letters of the Tetragrammaton, are sometimes used in his works as an acronym to refer to the sixth day (***Y****om* ***H****ashishi*) of creation and to Jesus who was crucified on that day. Thus, in hindsight, what is implied here is that during those fifteen years Abulafia was caught up in a struggle between his intellect and imagination, and that most of what happened had been driven by the imagination interpreting his visionary experiences rather than his intellect. In other words, as he put it in a later work, his soul or intellect had not yet become strong enough to "guard itself from the misleading images," including, perhaps, a Christian-based understanding of history and his mission, which led him astray.[35] And although God seemingly guided him during this period as is indicated by the letter notation *aleph-lamed-mem-heh,* which spells out *Elohim*—another of the Divine names—when the last two letters are reversed, a significant letter, *yod,* is missing, indicating that something was lacking. Hence, it is only at the end of this fifteen-year period that his eyes were opened and intellect finally overcame imagination.[36] This is also supported by the continuation of the passage, where Abulafia comments: "And I know, that were it not for the accidents of the imagination that I saw in my first visions, which, thank God, are now a thing of the past, my students would not have deserted me.[37] And those very phantasms . . . were Divine causes to teach me about my character and to successfully pass trials. . . ."[38] Abulafia recognizes that the visions of that first period were actually Divine tests designed to allow him to discover his true character, and prepare him for his ultimate role.

Thus, the many visions with apocalyptic undertones that Abulafia relates in the works written during this fifteen-year period, and which caused him to embark on a course of action leading him to Rome in 1280, from the perspective of hindsight may have been a misinterpretation of the Divine will. Abulafia seems to suggest in this paragraph, that though the visions themselves were of Divine origin, though he believed that he was interpreting them correctly, this was not the case. He also writes that his mission was to bring the "second curse" to a conclusion, meaning, as he implies elsewhere, that he was to announce the impending end of the power of Christianity and bring the exile to a close.[39] This reading is supported by the type of activities he was engaged in during this period, and by his continuous interaction with Christians, something that emerges from within his works.

When not seen with hindsight, but through the medium of the works Abulafia wrote in this period, this was a very intense and exciting time. It is difficult to know where Abulafia was geographically in the first five years, though it is a pretty safe guess that most of it was spent in Italy and Sicily. It is probable that he also spent time in Castile in the towns of Burgos and Medinaceli. It is during this period that Abulafia discovered the potential of *Sefer Yetzira* along with the teachings of the Ashkenazi pietists as a key to understanding the Torah, and started to develop his own unique interpretation.[40] This knowledge is also combined with Abulafia's reading of Maimonides' *Guide* and the uncovering of the secrets hidden within. It is probably during this period that Abulafia had Judah Salmon, Joseph Gikatilla, and Moses ben Simon of Burgos among his students.[41] It is also relatively certain that he spent some time with the Jewish community in Rome where he taught the *Guide* to Zedekiah ben Benjamin Anaw, a member of one of the leading Roman Jewish families, and to Rabbi Yeshayah of Trani, a leading Halachic authority.[42] In 1273, Abulafia wrote the first of three commentaries on the *Guide* entitled *Sefer ha-Geulah* (Book of Redemption) which was also one of the first Abulafian works to be translated into Latin by Flavius Mithridates for Pico della Mirandola in the fifteenth century.[43]

Prior to this Abulafia had written *Get ha-Shemot* and *Mafteah ha-Ra'ayon* in which he set out his visionary understanding of the Divine names and letters of the alphabet. In August or September 1276 (Elul 5036), a couple of months before the crucial vision, he wrote *Sefer ha-Melamed*, of which only the last part is extant, and which seems to deal with the Divine names while also clarifying certain statements in the *Guide.*[44] From the start, the centrality of the Tetragrammaton to Abulafia's thought is evident and given Abulafia's acquaintance with the works of the Ashkenazi pietists, this is not surprising.[45] However, what is immediately apparent from these works is that no connection is made between the Messiah, redemption, and the Tetragrammaton, there is a total lack of apocalyptic and messianic elements, and they are more straightforward, clearer, and easier to read.[46] This goes a long way to explaining the nature of the vision in 1270, which presumably gave him the insight to interpret *Sefer Yetzirah* and through the latter, discover the secrets about the names of God, letter combination, prophetic elevation, and the nature of creation.

And then, on the fifth of Tevet (Saturday, December 12, 1276) six years after leaving Barcelona, he received a vision, which clarified the secrets of the Divine name and the essence of prophecy.[47] It is worth citing a large portion of the text as reported in his commentary to a prophetic work, itself not extant:

> And after that, Raziel saw a vision in which he acquired the secret of the Name, the secret of prophecy and its true essence. And he said, in the time of *heh* (five) from his arrival in Dibon, it being the *vav* (sixth) year since he left Spain, in *yud* (ten), which is the month called Tevet, on its *heh* (fifth) day, behold he discovered the Name of God. . . . And then he began with the Name—Raziel said: "The Lord my God sent His angel before me who showed me the ways of His Name, and I saw from within It, ten Divine visions, and the tenth vision was like the first, and the voice of the Almighty emerging from between the two, and I was petrified when I heard the voice. And I understood ten things from one voice, and seven tongues in each and every one of them" . . . and with this secret Raziel sealed (t)his book with four words, their first letters spelling *YHWH* and their last letters *THLT* and their secret: the knowledge of the messiah and the wisdom of the redeemer (*YediaT Hamashiah Ve-hochmaT Ha-goeL*), the beginning (*teḥilat*) of the being (*havayah*) of I (*ego*) wisdom (*ḥacham*), my name (*shemi*) is my witness (*edi*).[48]

This vision, which took place on an auspicious day signified by the letters of the Tetragrammaton, revealed to Abulafia the full meaning of the Divine name and he understood that his messianic career was about to begin. The seal at the end of the book signals the start of the reign of this Divine name, implicitly connected with redemption and the Messiah. The Messiah is revealed by the acronym formed with the letters of the Tetragrammaton, and the last letters of the acronym signal its beginning in history. The middle letters of each of the four words (*YediaT Ha-mashiaH Ve-hochmaT Ha-goeL*) emphasize even more clearly that the Messiah is Abulafia himself as witnessed by the last sentence of the quotation. The first two words (*YHWH* and *THLT*) are the first and last letters of the four word seal and the last four words are the remaining letters of each of the four words.[49] The description of the revelation itself, particularly in the matter of the Divine speech, is reminiscent of midrashic statements regarding the giving of the Torah at Sinai. What seems to be implied in the way Abulafia describes the experience is that the ten visions are parallel to the Decalogue (or the sefirot?), but that in this case, it is an understanding that is not exclusive to the children of Israel, but is revealed in seventy tongues, in other words, for all the nations of the world. Abulafia's interpretation of this vision becomes clear in the course of the next few years where he does not restrict his messianic activities to Jews alone.[50]

Thus, it is from this date that Abulafia's messianic career started. The tone and nature of his writing changed entirely, he was constantly on the move as he was actively missionizing, and it is during this period that we find the first predictions about the end of time, and Abulafia's own claim to be the Messiah. These books and indeed the vision itself can only be understood against the backdrop of his interaction with Christians, particularly those of a Joachimite bent.[51] It is surely reasonable to presume that during his wanderings in southern Italy and Sicily, Abulafia met these figures, and their conversations inspired him to interpret his life in a messianic context, and the visions he had as a Divine command to proselytize, leading eventually to Rome to see the pope in 1280. He understood that the end of Christian domination was nigh and that he had been given knowledge of the Divine name that would bring about the redemption. The date of this redemption was also clear: it was a period of ten years that would start with his audience with the pope on the eve of the Jewish New Year in 1280 (the start of 5041 AM) and would culminate ten years later in apocalyptic grandeur with the full revelation of the Messiah and recognition by all the faiths of the knowledge of the true Divine name.[52]

Abulafia spent some time in Greece in the towns of Patras and Thebes teaching the secrets of the *Guide* and his messianic vision. Then in 1279, awakened by Divine revelation that the time was right, he started to make his way slowly to Rome. He stayed for a while in Capua where he probably wrote *Hayei ha-Nefesh* (Life of the Soul), the second of his commentaries on the *Guide.* It is clear that his ideas were provoking controversy as Abulafia mentions forces in Capua trying to dissuade people from listening to him. He then proceeded to Trani where the Jewish community informed on him to the Christian authorities, who had him imprisoned. This is not surprising given that Abulafia was probably very upfront about his intentions, and since 1270, the communities of southern Italy had faced sustained pressure from apostates and the Dominicans, and were trying to keep a low profile. Times were changing for the Jews of southern Italy as the mendicants were making their presence known, and there would be mass (forced) conversions of many of the communities just ten years later.[53] The community would not have wanted to draw attention to themselves, and Abulafia's messianic claims along with his well-publicized intention to see the pope would not have been welcomed. Detained in Trani, what Abulafia calls a miracle, perhaps the intervention of Franciscan friars, took place and he was freed and allowed to make his way to Rome.[54] The buildup to his expected meeting with Nicholas III, the latter's refusal to meet with Abulafia, and his sudden death and the aftermath will be discussed in much greater detail in a later chapter. However, what seems immediately apparent is that there were elements within the Christian world who encouraged him in his mission. This is unlikely to have been because they accepted his teachings at face value; more probably because they saw Abulafia as part and parcel of the process leading up to the apocalyptic events they envisioned starting in Italy in the period leading up to 1290.[55]

Following the episode in Rome, Abulafia made his way back to Capua where he wrote *Sitrei Torah* (Secrets of the Torah), the third of his commentaries on the *Guide of the Perplexed,* for four of his students.[56] Also in this period, he wrote his most popular work (judging by the number of extant manuscripts) *Hayei ha-Olam ha-Ba* (Life in the World to Come), which is a manual for achieving prophetic revelation, and a number of prophetic works that are not extant.[57] What are extant are a series of very enigmatic commentaries (containing quotations from the originals), that he himself wrote to these works in 1282–1283 after the remarkable events at Rome, which exhibit messianic traits and apocalyptic excitement. He clearly believes that he is the Messiah who will finally be recognized by Jews and Christians in 1290, and though he was going through a very difficult period, shunned by both Jews and Christians, all will finally come right. He has a number of disciples whom he mentions in some of his works but, in the main, is having difficulty convincing people of the truth of his teachings. This does not stop him from preaching and spreading his apocalyptic message everywhere he can, and not only to Jews but to Christians as well.[58] Indeed, Abulafia makes reference to conversations he had with discerning Christians, perhaps a reference to the Franciscan Joachimites, who were convinced that there was a truer more perfect knowledge of the Torah than that found in the Gospels. Jesus and his disciples had taught with the purpose of attracting the masses to belief, but the inner meaning of the Torah aimed at prophetic perfection.[59]

In one of his prophetic works written during this period of intense activity, Abulafia emphatically states that it was God who commanded him to turn to the Christian world. From the context, it is clear that Abulafia informed them of the impending end of the power of Christianity in this world, and though some believed him, Abulafia writes that they "did not return to YHWH because they trusted in their swords and bows."[60] The Christian response might reflect the belief that they would be able to counter the forces of the Antichrist by conventional means and that though they believed that the end of the world was fast approaching, they would prevail as promised in Revelation.

While Abulafia's attitude toward Christianity will be dealt with in greater detail later, in this context it is interesting to note that in the second part of an apocalyptic prophetic book that describes his life as a messianic figure, *Sefer ha-Ot* (Book of the Sign), where he openly makes mention of his mission to the Christians, Abulafia refers to himself as Zecharyahu.[61] Zecharyahu is the name of the biblical prophet of redemption, Zachariah, with a *vav* added at the end to make it numerically equal to Abraham (248). There he talks about himself being sent to the poor, and to Jews and Christians.[62] As discussed in the previous chapter, in the anonymous *Vita* written by a Florensian a few years after his death in 1202, Joachim's whole career is centered around his prophetic visions, his ability to tell the future, and his being a model of the biblical prophets of the exile, Ezekiel and Jeremiah.[63] Abulafia's adoption of Zachariah may be a reflection of the polemical dialogue he was engaged in with the Franciscans. He uses the image of the one prophet who talks about redemption to counter the image of the other prophets who talk about the expected doom. Both Joachim and Abulafia talk about a progression to spiritual knowledge, and Abulafia expressly mentions that his preaching is directed to the poor, which would strongly resonate with these elements within the Franciscan Order.[64] In addition, according to the anonymous *Vita,* Joachim's visit to the Holy Land and his criticism of the religious there caused him to believe that the geographical location of the new Holy Land where the seeds of the third status would be sown would be Calabria and southern Italy. Abulafia also plays down the geographical significance of the Holy Land, particularly in the context of prophecy and the spiritual redemption that he promulgates through knowledge of the Name. For him, the new Holy Land and the place where the Messiah was to be revealed was Sicily.[65]

It is also during this period that the Jewish community turned up the pressure and a campaign against Abulafia was instigated by leaders of the community in Sicily and spearheaded by the leading Halachic authority in the Crown of Aragon, Rabbi Solomon ibn Adret. A record of these travails also appears in the second section of *Sefer ha-Ot* written in 1284. At this juncture Abulafia had been forced to take refuge on an uninhabited island, Comnino, just off the coast of the island of Malta because of the campaign being waged against him.[66] It seems that some of the leaders of the community in Palermo had written to Barcelona to ask for advice regarding Abulafia. Though the letter is not extant, it stands to reason that it was written in the aftermath of the Sicilian Vespers of 1282, which started a twenty-year war that only ended with the signing of the Treaty of Caltabellotta in 1302.[67] In a pretty unstable political environment, a Jew claiming to be the Messiah and a prophet and openly preaching to Jews and Christians about the impending end of Christianity might not have been exactly what the community needed, and they wanted to know whether Abulafia's claims were credible.

In *Ve-Zot le-Yehudah* (And this is for Judah), a letter written after 1285 to Judah Salmon, a disciple of his in Barcelona, Abulafia attempted to show that he had the requisite background for what he was preaching and that he was more qualified than his detractors. Abulafia defends himself against what he thought was a vicious smear campaign against his person and teachings by the aforementioned leader of the community in Catalonia, Solomon ibn Adret.[68] The latter had written a harsh letter to Rabbi Ahitub of Palermo, who was actually Abulafia's disciple and one of those for whom the latter wrote his Torah commentary, probably to discover the nature of his relationship with Abulafia and to negate his prophetic and messianic claims.[69] Rabbi Ahitub likely showed the letter to his teacher who was so distressed that he put pen to paper in order to clear his name and teachings in Barcelona.[70] Abulafia's response to ibn Adret's letter is very important because he provides a lot of information about his intellectual formation. He had to show his accreditation, and therefore goes into great detail about what he had studied in order to demonstrate that his revelations could be trusted. He shows that he understands sefirotic Kabbalah but takes it one step farther and merges it with his prophetic Kabbalah, which he claims is beyond the capabilities of philosophers or theosophical Kabbalists. However, Ibn Adret proved to be unimpressed and acted decisively against Abulafia placing a ban on him along with another self-proclaimed prophet in Avila.

One of Solomon ibn Adret's main concerns with Abulafia was the question of prophecy. Rabbinic tradition, from the Midrash to Judah ha-Levi and Nahmanides held that prophecy was intimately connected with the Land of Israel. Claims for prophetic capabilities when coupled with apocalyptic messianic ideology were incredibly dangerous and risked undermining the authority of the rabbis. Hence, in his letter dealing with Abulafia, ibn Adret referred to him as "that trickster, may the name of the wicked rot, Abraham, who set himself up as prophet and messiah in Sicily, who seduced with his falsehoods some of the children of Israel, and had I not slammed the door in his face by the mercy of God, with his imaginary and false teachings, he almost got going and would have annihilated [the community] . . ."[71] Abulafia's defense of his prophetic capabilities is found in a number of places. In *Sefer ha-Ḥeshek* (Book of Desire) he neutralizes the importance of the geographic location of the Land of Israel, explaining that the Land refers to the descent of the Divine presence on a person who is deserving of it.[72] However, in his commentary on Exodus, Abulafia takes a different tack, showing that Sicily is a place where prophecy is possible: "The secret of Sicily is *Aryeh* (Lion), 'At the mountain of the Lord He will be seen (*yeraeh*)' . . . hints at the *'y ha-rei* (Island of Rei) because *'y ha-rei* has *aleph yud* on both sides, hinting at half the alphabet (*aleph* and *yud* in gematria equal eleven, and there are twenty-two letters in the Hebrew alphabet), and *heh resh* (also the Hebrew for mountain) in the middle, and its secret is down and up, up and down (*matah u-maala maala u-matah*)."[73] Sicily, *Aryeh* and *ha-rei* (an anagram of *Aryeh*) have the same numerical value of 219. The lion is the symbol of the tribe of Judah representing kingship and the seed of the Messiah. The verse from Genesis 22:14 that refers to the mountain where Abraham almost sacrificed Isaac is the place of revelation. When the order of the letters of *Aryeh* are changed, we get the word *yeraeh* and if the order is changed again *ha-rei* which is the name Abulafia gives to Sicily. Thus, the Torah already hints at the Abraham who will prophesy on the Island of Sicily using the letters of the Hebrew alphabet. Abulafia's name for Sicily also incorporates the *har*—the mountain, as in the verse from Genesis, which is numerically equal to "down and up, up and down" implying prophetic experience. Thus, Abulafia is at pains to defend the legitimacy of his prophesying, apocalyptic visions, and messianic expectations.

It is unclear when Abulafia left the island of Comnino, but in late 1285 he was in Messina where he wrote *Otzar Eden Ganuz*.[74] This work signals a major change in Abulafia's perception of his life and mission, though not in his apocalyptic thought. It is immediately noticeable that in the biographical passage cited earlier in this chapter, there is no mention whatsoever of Abulafia's attempt to meet with the pope. An event of such magnitude, which was described in detail in a prophetic work incorporating visions that were part of the whole experience, was now totally ignored. Yet, when the passage is read carefully, one realizes that it presents a spiritual biography, rather than a real *curriculum vita,* and what Abulafia wanted to show is that he had finally attained the "seal within the seal," the highest level of spiritual comprehension, true prophecy.[75] Indeed, the biographical details can only be understood when seen in the context of what follows in the book. Abulafia sets out the truest innermost way of reading the biblical text, which is in itself prophecy. This attainment is described as entering the holy of holies and is called the seventh path.[76] From the manner in which this path is set out by Abulafia, this was clearly a major breakthrough and brought about a significant change in how he perceived himself and his divinely inspired mission. The messianic elements so central in the last decade or so are still present, but they are more subtly portrayed. Abulafia still knows that the end is near and expects it to happen in 1290, but his own role is now more muted. No longer does he talk of himself in openly apocalyptic language as the expected Messiah, but as someone who has achieved the highest level of mystical cognition and spiritual understanding, and as one who has a duty to teach these matters to those capable of comprehending them. Abulafia concentrates on teaching the various elements of his Kabbalistic system, which are the stepping stones to prophecy and knowledge of the Divine name. He also becomes far more selective about his students and, seemingly, he has almost no further contact with

Christians, though Christianity and its place in the Divine schema still play a significant role in his thought.

Abulafia's movements during these years are unclear, though it is probable that he remained in the general area of Sicily and southern Italy. He was quite prolific and composed, among other things, a commentary on sections of each of the five books of the Torah, and a number of books in which he elucidates how to achieve the level of prophecy. He also wrote the aforementioned *Ve-Zot le-Yehudah* and another letter, *Sheva Netivot ha-Torah* (Seven Paths of the Torah), which are important, as they are apologetic in nature and give some indication about his state of mind during this period. That he felt under siege can also be seen from the vitriolic introduction to the *Otzar Eden Ganuz*. There Abulafia rails against those who focus on the Halachah and material things, those who have forgotten the roots and basis of belief. He also criticizes those who choose to ignore his teachings and who spread slander against him.[77] These comments together with his epistles are surely a reflection of the campaign spearheaded against him from Barcelona.

However, even given Solomon ibn Adret's vitriolic remarks against Abulafia, it is possible that there is some evidence that his claim to be a messianic contender had adherents in the Crown of Aragon as well as in Sicily. In May 1286, a series of disputations between a Genoese Christian, Inghetto Contardo, and various Jews took place in Majorca. Though the text was written in Genoa at a later date, there is good reason to believe that it reflects events that actually occurred. During one of these encounters with a Jewish "Magister," Inghetto cites Daniel 12:11–12 as referring to the false messiah who will reign for three and a half years, which is one thousand two hundred and ninety days. The Jewish Magister replies that "[t]his is a good belief and I believe that this is what will be. And I say to you that if it does not happen after 1290, I will know what I have to do, and it is a short time from now, it being but four years away."[78] The Magister apparently interprets the verse from Daniel as referring to years not days, and clearly expects the Messiah to come in 1290. This could reflect belief that Abulafia was indeed the Messiah and perhaps indicates that there were those who supported him and were waiting with intense expectation for the end of days.

The period leading up to 1290 would not have been a very pleasant one for the Jews in southern Italy and its dependencies. The Dominicans, with the passive cooperation of the Anjevin ruler's dependency on the papacy, had embarked on a preaching campaign aimed at converting Jews, which eventually resulted in mass conversions in the early 1290s.[79] Following the Sicilian Vespers, things were different in Sicily itself, but Abulafia would have still been under immense pressure from leaders of the Jewish community who did not like his teachings or what they considered his disrupting influence. This is reflected in *Sheva Netivot ha-Torah* written in 1290 to Abraham, possibly a disciple of his in Messina. In the letter, he maps out the steps leading to the highest level of prophecy, and analyzes the differences between his system and that of the theosophical Kabbalists of Catalonia. While this epistle is a result of these continued attacks against his teachings and reflects his need to retaliate and defend himself against his detractors, it also serves as an indication of where he envisioned himself within the framework of events leading up to the fast approaching end of days.

Toward the end of the letter, Abulafia makes reference to the redemption, but states that at present, because he is being persecuted, he is currently unable to find the necessary isolation, and presumably peace of mind, needed to prophesy.[80] Thus, though there does not seem to have been any change in the apocalyptic timetable, Abulafia seems unsure about things, and tries to calm the choppy waters by clearly showing why his teachings are superior to all other forms of knowledge. The epistle sets out the seven levels of learning, the seventh and highest being the achievement of prophecy, based on the combination of letters and knowledge of the Divine name, a level that he only understood fully in late 1285. Abulafia shows that his method of reading the Torah leading to prophecy based on *Sefer Yetzira* is the correct way, and it was used by the ancient rabbis as well.[81] He brings proof texts from the Talmud and Midrash to show that the use he makes of gematria, letter combination, and acrostics is more important than any kind of philosophical approach and leads to true knowledge of the Divine name.[82] He goes to great lengths to show the superiority of *hochmat ha-tzeruf* over all other forms of knowledge.[83] Abulafia denigrates those whom he refers to as "Masters of the Names," saying that their use of letter combinations to achieve magical ends is false and is very different from his Kabbalah.[84] This again might be a reflection of one of the complaints against his teaching, and a reason for his continued persecution.

In late 1287, Abulafia wrote the third and most apocalyptic section of *Sefer ha-Ot* (Book of the Sign). This section depicts events that are expected to happen in the near future and which are initialized by a warrior come to fight the wars of the Lord leading a host numbering twenty-two thousand (presumably representing the twenty-two letters of the Hebrew alphabet). This man has a sign of a white letter with marks of blood and ink either side of it inscribed in his forehead. The sign is very powerful and inspires Abulafia to write the book which he is then commanded to send to Spain, again, perhaps, reflecting the nature of the forces arraigned against him.[85] Having blessed Abulafia, the man with the sign disappears, and he has a vision of a war fought between three great men who come from different corners of the earth. This vision is explained to Abulafia by an old man named Yehoel sitting on a chair on the mountain of judgment wearing crimson robes, who explains that the three men represent three kings and kingdoms, and that he, the fourth king is, it seems, the guardian of the children of Israel. The expected Messiah will be the fifth who is soon to come.[86]

Though not explicitly referring to himself as the expected fifth king, Abulafia still clearly viewed himself as the Messiah. In his commentary on the Torah written in 1288–1289, Abulafia referred to himself as being crucified on the Tree of Life and Death for eighteen years with two more still to go. And in another section of the work dealing with criteria for recognizing a prophet and the Messiah, he reiterates that the latter is about to appear, and from the description of his character, it is not hard to guess the expected Messiah's identity.[87] However, the days of active messianic activity in preparation for the coming eschaton are noticeably absent, and it seems that Abulafia understood that he would only be revealed in his full glory at the end of days. In the works written during this period, Abulafia mainly concentrates on teaching the essence of the Divine name, knowledge of which is an essential part of the eschaton, and on the hermeneutical methods by which one can have true knowledge of the Torah and attain prophecy.

Abulafia's relations with his students were problematic. His expectations were clearly very high indeed, and not many of those attracted to his teachings were able to stay the course. In *Otzar Eden Ganuz* he gives a long list of places that he visited and the students that he had in each place with comments about their respective abilities. The list contains far more records of failure than success.[88] Abulafia also wrote books for his disciples. One example is a book completed on March 13, 1287, which deals with the priestly blessing that for Abulafia contains the secret of prophecy. The book was written, aptly, for Solomon ha-Cohen (the priest) who was originally from the Holy Land. The latter had asked Abulafia to explain the secret true meaning of the priestly blessing so that when required to do so, he, from a family of priestly descent, would be able to do it with the correct intention.[89] Abulafia wrote *Sefer ha-Heshek,* a book that focuses on the Divine name in Messina for one of his favourite disciples Sa'adia b. Isaac Galmasi and another disciple called Jacob ben Abraham.[90] Abulafia wrote *Or ha-Sechel* (Light of the Intellect) in Messina probably in 1285 for Abraham ben Shalom Comti and Natan b. Saadia Harar.[91]

However, his disciples are also instrumental for his messianic tasks and bear witness to his prophesying in Sicily in the period after 1285. This is evident from his aforementioned commentary on the Torah, particularly the section dealing with the exodus from Egypt, which signifies the future redemption. Seven disciples are mentioned by name in this context, three of them—Saadia b. Isaac Galmasi, Abraham b. Shalom Comti, and Natan b. Saadia Harar mentioned above—are in Messina, and four—Ahitub b. Isaac, his brother David, Solomon b. Yachin, and Solomon b. David—are in Palermo.[92] According to the commentary, the secret of Messina is a cloud (*anan*) and the month of Nissan, the month of redemption (all three have a numerical value of 170), while the secret of Palermo is dust (*afar,* both 350 numerically) representing matter.[93] Thus, the three who are in Messina are witnesses to the hidden one who prophesies, that is, Abulafia himself, while the four in Palermo, connected to the material world, bear witness to the power of the name which is both one and three (presumably based on Deut. 6:4). The seven students also symbolize the seven lower sefirot, and the two representations of the letter *shin* on opposite sides of the phylacteries worn on the head, one of which has three branches, the other four. Thus, they have a central role to play in bringing about the redemption and connecting the Divine spiritual world with this material one.

The last work that Abulafia wrote was *Imrei Shefer* (Sayings of Wisdom), which is a manual for attaining prophecy and true knowledge of the Divine name. In the book, Abulafia says that he is in the twenty-first year of his knowledge of the Divine name, the year now being 5051, and that from 5039 (1279) he had been busy writing books about this knowledge, as we have already seen.[94] This is the last biographical piece of information that we have regarding Abulafia, and we are left to speculate as to his end. Clearly, for a long time Abulafia believed that he would be revealed as Messiah by the end of the Jewish year 5050 which ended in early September 1290. However, in his Torah commentary, Abulafia seems to suggest that his messiahship might come to fruition during 5051. Interestingly, this correlates nicely with a comment made in *Sefer ha-Edut* (Book of Testimony), where it is implied that the redemption from those who worship the moon (Muslims?) will take place in Tishrei (ca. September), but the redemption from those who worship the sun (Christians) will take place in Nissan (ca. March).[95] In the Mediterranean world of this period, the new calendar year did not start, as it does today, in January, but usually in March, and in 1291, the beginning of the month of Nissan fell at the start of March.[96] Hence, it could very well be that Abulafia believed that he would be revealed as Messiah at the end of 5050, but the full redemption from Christianity would only happen in Nissan 5051

(March 25, 1291—the start of the new calendar year corresponding to 23 Nissan, immediately following Passover).[97] *Imre Shefer* was evidently written during this six month period, and in preparation for the momentous events that were about to occur. One can only imagine Abulafia's disappointment in March 1291 when the expected events did not come to pass. While this does not help in solving the mystery surrounding Abulafia's vanishing act, it might go some way to explaining the reasons for it.

The Politics of Universal Salvation

In many places in his works, Abulafia cites the start of Nahmanides' Torah commentary where he writes that the whole Torah is made up of the names of God.[1] This provides Abulafia with his justification to read the Torah not according to the text as we have it, but to find within it the Divine names and the true inner meaning of the text. This he claims was what was revealed to Moses and is the reason for the Torah starting from the story of creation.[2] According to Abulafia, Maimonides revealed these matters in his *Guide for the Perplexed* for those who were capable of understanding them. Even though Maimonides, at the start of the third section of the *Guide,* hints against revealing things that should remain secret, Abulafia writes that because the end of days is nigh and the Divine efflux is strongly felt, it is a time of increased spiritual comprehension for many. In addition, he feels that it is his job to awaken those who do not yet recognize that the end of days is fast approaching. In its three parts, the *Guide* contains within it thirty-six secrets and Abulafia's commentaries are designed to present them.

In the introduction to *Sitrei Torah,* composed in Capua in 1280, the last of his three commentaries to the *Guide,* Abulafia presents the rationale behind using the method of letter combinations to read the Torah.[3] It reveals the innermost and truest hermeneutical reading of the Torah divinely revealed to Moses by the Active Intellect and is the reason why the Torah will never be replaced by another.[4] Moses presented the Torah on two levels: the straightforward simple reading of the Torah and the Commandments, which is supplemented by the oral law, and the secret inner reading of the Torah, which reveals the Divine names and the true purpose of the

Commandments. Abulafia implies here that the former is for those not capable of comprehending the latter, and the latter does not include the oral law per se, but is based only on the Torah itself which includes within it all reality. It is also a reading that can only be revealed in the time immediately preceding the coming of the Messiah. Abulafia writes: "And for this reason, it is impossible that this Torah can be ignored or that any other should come in its place. However, it is certain and definite that its secrets will be revealed in the time of the Messiah by the prophets who will arise, and by the Messiah himself. For with it [the Torah] will all of Israel and those who attach themselves become knowledgeable as it is written: 'For all will know me from their youngsters to their elders' (Jeremiah 31:32) and 'For the knowledge of YHVH will fill the world as water fills the sea' (Isaiah 11:9)."[5] In the context of a Joachimite milieu, this comment is fascinating as it suggests a similar methodology for reading the biblical text as the key for true knowledge, and also implies that there will not be a new revelation at the end of times, but a different, truer, understanding of the same text, which is open to all who wish to embrace it.

At the end of his commentary to the prophetic book *Sefer ha-Edut* Abulafia writes: "The seal of the exile of Israel is complete, and the reason is because the true Name has been revealed. . . . And he [Abulafia] said: the blood of Israel is demanded (*nidrash*) and the reign of the fourth beast is completed. . . . And it is all the seal of truth (*emet*), you (*atem*) are also the children of Israel. Be reconciled with us now, so that the acclaimed Temple can be built."[6] For Abulafia, the events in Rome in 1280 signaled the end of the reign of the fourth kingdom, and the fourth beast, which had ravaged the earth persecuting Israel, was now finally vanquished.[7] The length of the exile, set out in Daniel 7, determined as "a time, two times and half a time," was over, and with the renewed revelation of the name, a new age was about to start. The seal of truth (*emet*) reveals that the reign of the fourth beast had ended after 5040 years, which implies that all of mankind had in essence been in exile, non-Jews included.[8] Abulafia's contention seems to be that the Christians are also part of Israel, part of the truth (*emet*), and there needs to be a process of reconciliation, not retribution, so that a new temple, presumably for all peoples, can be constructed.[9] Abulafia's ideal was of universal redemption and perfection, regardless of religion, in the knowledge of God through knowledge of the Holy Name.

Abulafia's views on the economy of salvation, the relationship between Jews and Gentiles, and who is capable of knowing the Divine name which is the ultimate truth and purpose of creation and being, are predicated on a sophisticated understanding of the reasons for the emergence of the different nations, languages, scripts, and religions in history. He sets out these views in a number of places in his works, but nowhere more clearly than in the works he wrote in late 1285. The latter part of this year was, as has already been noted, a very creative period in Abulafia's life where he seems to have understood with much greater clarity issues that were troubling him earlier. *Otzar Eden Ganuz,* one of the longest works Abulafia wrote, culminates with a biographical passage that was intended to show that he had achieved the highest level of wisdom and knowledge, the seventh of the paths that he later sets out in *Sheva netivot ha-Torah* written in 1290. The structure of the book leads to its conclusion, but already in the introduction of this work, Abulafia informs the reader that its purpose is get at the very essence of faith which is the knowledge of the true Torah, or in other words, knowledge of the Divine name. Thus, the first part of the book is a commentary on *Sefer Yetzirah* (Book of Creation) which also deals with history and teleology. The second part deals with time within the context of history, and the third part, which starts off in a Maimonidean fashion, deals with knowledge of the Divine names. It is Abulafia's portrayal of the teleological progression of humanity through his understanding of the structure and nature of creation and its relationship with God, which will be indicative of the connection between these ideas and the particular historical context in which they were elaborated.

Abulafia starts out from the general premise that everything and all beings are part of the Divine creation, and that the whole creation bears witness to the Creator. There is a hierarchical chain of being whereby a lesser being is acted upon by its superior. For instance, the body, soul, and intellect of man are a microcosm which exemplify the macrocosm, in that the intellect acts on the soul and through it on the body, as does God, the Prime Mover, act, via the spheres and Active Intellect, on the ever-changing present. The starting point for comprehending the Divine being is the natural world, which was created in order that God's perfection and munificence would be witnessed by humans. The incredible variety in creation from inanimate objects to the most complex of beings, man, are all interlinked in a chain that stretches all the way back to God, and each of the species in its own way and according to its natural ability receives the Divine efflux. The incredible diversity of types of created species also illustrates the necessity for variety and difference within each of the species, even though every existent being can be linguistically referred to as the same thing—as something created. Even if humans can all essentially be referred to as mankind, the very existence of individuals who think and act differently from each other predicates that in the same manner that the body is made up of many individual parts that function together, humans will necessarily form social groupings.

Abulafia writes:

> And the differences between nations is predicated on reasons different from those which explain the variety of created beings . . . and the reasons for the differences between nations, religions, languages, and script are all intimately connected. And it is known that if change of place and time is primarily responsible for the difference between nations, hence, it will also be the reason for the different religions. And one could also invert this saying that the differences in religious belief are the reason for there being different nations. However, because we are aware that there are very different kinds of peoples, some of whom lack any religion whatsoever, one would have to surmise that the formation of nations preceded the division and divergence of religions. And while this is a conclusion reached by way of reason, it is substantiated from the (section of the) Torah dealing with Noah and the generation of the flood,

> where nations were divided one from the other, and as is well known, the Torah was not given until the time of Moses, and all the other religions emerge from the Torah.
>
> And behold the laws which distinguish one nation from another always existed, and they are to our species as morals are to man, different from one another. And the Torah teaches us that the differences in languages and ways of speech were also necessary when the nations were differentiated one from the other. However, the different scripts were elaborated for the preservation of the religions, and the different scripts are indicators of the various languages, religions and peoples . . .
>
> And we will say that what is sufficient to believe in this matter is that the differences between humans are the reason for the variety of nations, and the variety of nations are the cause of different religions, and the differences between the religions, which explains why there are different customs and laws, are responsible for the different languages which are responsible for the various scripts. And all these changes explain why people think differently, which also explains the variety of opinions and beliefs, and all of these previous factors together explain why people act in different ways . . .[10]

Abulafia says that each of these differences has to be examined carefully, and explains why it is a natural choice for humans to be part of societies. While all humans are alike in essence each one has an individual personality and intellect. The intellect is the guiding force of each individual allowing him, if he is capable, to achieve the ultimate goal, which is knowledge of the Divine name. In the same manner that the individual human who is made up of so many diverse parts, needs the intellect to unite and direct the whole, thus does the human species, consisting of many individuals who, naturally, cohere into collectives or nations, require leaders. These leaders, whether they be king, wise man, or prophet, will be able to lead a great number of their constituents to achieve the ultimate goal, which is "becoming united with the Active Intellect which transmits the Divine efflux (*ha-Kabbalah ha-Elohit*) to those who search for it, which is the cause of internal life for those who receive it. . . ."[11] What emerges is that every human being of whatever nation or faith is capable of achieving man's ultimate goal which is *unio mystica*.

In addition, each nation will have its own unique laws and religion with its obligations which will be the basis for achieving the desired end. Because each leader will want to show his independence from his predecessor, he will develop a unique script, which, according to Abulafia, is in essence the same as the original script in that it is still letter combinations, but it has different accidental properties. So, for example, in Hebrew, the letters *Aleph Dalet Mem* (*Adam*) refer to a person, and in Greek, the leader who developed the script chose letters that make up the word *anthropos,* and in Latin *homo,* but they all refer to the same thing—man. In other words, because the essence of all languages based on the combination of letters is the same, there is no substantial difference between the words used in the different languages to refer to the same thing. Abulafia continues: "And on this matter we can say that all who follow our teaching which is grasped by prophecy will know that the easiest way of attaining the truth of reality is by the combination of letters; and even though one can perceive reality by way of the intellect, the way to apprehend it is by letter combination."[12]

Returning to the leader, Abulafia says that sometimes he will utilize the knowledge of his predecessors, but will interpret their words in ways that suit his purpose, or he will totally ignore them in order to develop his own path.

> And for this reason, he will have to distance his nation from all others, and he will frighten them with all manner of punishment if they try to mix with other peoples. He will also promise them rewards if they keep the law that has been lain down by the leader, and pledge that only they, and those like them and those who join them will inherit the world to come while all other nations will go to hell. And the leaders of the people emphasise these matters via their particular religion, language and script, creating a desire from youth to old age so that these laws will be retained, taught, and passed down from generation to generation for eternity.[13]

In other words, Abulafia is implying that all nations are constructs of leaders who in their great wisdom perceive the ultimate truth, and try to transmit this knowledge to their citizens by creating their own myths. Each nation has its own particularities and exclusiveness in order to sustain this natural, but also divinely ordained, framework and organization of humanity. The language, script, and religion are the tools by which the leaders of the nations do this, and while, superficially, it may seem that there are great and irreconcilable differences between the different nations, they are all attempting to arrive at the same ultimate truth which is the basis of all human existence. This remarkable conclusion becomes even clearer when Abulafia writes: "And the differences between the nations are like the matters which divide between Jews, Christians and Muslims. And the differences between the religions are like the differences between the religion of Moses, the religion of Jesus and the religion of Muhammad, though in all three, the Divine name is necessarily unified, for there is no religion which does not teach the truth of [Divine] unity . . . and therefore, on the matter of [Divine] unity, there is no argument between us."[14]

This section concludes with the following insight, which explains with great clarity and logic why there is so much disagreement between the different peoples:

> And these differences which have been highlighted here are the reason for the variety of thoughts, opinions and deeds. For the variety of thoughts is more a matter of habit, than something natural. The lad who has been brought up in one of these thought systems, in other words, learned the script of his people till he could write very well, and all his speech was in the language of his people, and he internalised the religion, laws, customs and mannerisms; how is it possible to expect that he will think that any alternative path is not false. Or that he will consider the path of other people who do not follow his people's way to be true, and his own path all lies. Thus, it must be said, that it is obligatory that a person will only consider his way and that of his nation to be the true way, and that everything he has been taught to be true, and everything else to be false. For his intellect is submerged in a great sea, and his language does not know how to save him from drowning, because he has

> become habituated, and this is what leads him to affirm the truth of what he has received, whether it is true or false, for he is unable to measure it against anything else.[15]

If this is indeed the case, are there any objective criteria for knowing which of the nations or faiths is closer to the ultimate truth? Abulafia will, naturally, want to demonstrate that the Jewish people, its religion, language, and script are the best of all the nations and religions. However, he is aware that others will say that given the above reasoning, there was no possibility that he could admit anything else, given that he had been nurtured within the Jewish tradition! Abulafia suggests two, and only two, possible ways of determining between the religions. The first is utilizing the philosophical tools set out by Aristotle in his various works to distinguish truth and falsehood and apply them to the question at hand. If what a religion claims concurs with intuition (*regesh*) and reason, then these are good grounds for accepting its premises as true. The second, better, and ultimately conclusive way is via revelation, though Abulafia is aware of the difficulties involved here. He writes, however, "and it is obligatory on all those who have the ability to discern the truth to investigate, know and recognize it, in order to verify its true traditions, and peel away the imaginary matters which by necessity are transmitted to the vulgar crowd. And this is because of the deep profundity of the truth and the inability of most to comprehend it."[16] Divine revelation is the only way to escape human acculturation and perceive the truth not clouded by the frameworks of social grouping and organization.

Returning to the issue of which nation is the closest to God, Abulafia first shows that in the same way that in each of the three created worlds (the created part of the Divine world, the world of the heavens, and the material world) there is the most superior being (respectively, the first efflux, *Aravot*—the first of the seven heavens, and primal man) that excels above and encompasses everything else, thus, among the nations, there must also be one that excels above the rest. The matter can be decided by judging whether the laws, language, and script of a particular nation are the basis for those of all the other nations and whether the former inspire the most sublime thought and knowledge.

Abulafia suggests that in order to reach a conclusion on this issue, it is necessary to examine each nation from three different perspectives being "intellect, soul, and body":

> In other words, one has to examine whether their intellect is able to overcome the matters attaining to the soul, and if the soul overcomes bodily concerns, and whether the body has control over what is external to it, or vice versa. And these matters should be judged from the perspective of three general groups: the first are the best of the nation's intellectuals, in other words, those few scholars who know the secrets of the nation; those with the best souls, in other words, the righteous and wise men who fear sin; and the best physical specimens, in other words, those who are in control of their monetary affairs and love their bodies more than it [their money]. For these three types are among the best of any nation, and they are deserving of being part of the general species of mankind. . . . And it is known that man is only man because he is created in the image and shape of God. And these are the test cases from every nation which should be compared with other nations. And this is because any one of the nations who can exhibit the greatest perfection in these three test cases, is better than the other nations, by measure of the degree of its perfection against the others. And in this matter, there is no need for you to be biased about any nation, and even less so about your own nation, for the examination of truth among created beings is not determined by human will or choice, but is to know what are the things God has chosen in them which sets them apart from the others, and you should choose them as well, and do your utmost to follow them.[17]

Hence, this threefold division will give a sense of perspective to the person trying to establish which is the true faith and a way to measure the difference between the different religions. Yet even here, there can be disagreement as to which religion has the best of these three categories. However, Abulafia sees the division into the three descending degrees of Priesthood, Levites, and *Yahadut,* which he subsequently refers to as Israelites, as an indication that the Jewish, or Israelite, nation is the closest to God. Each of the three degrees within the nation have their own heads, respectively in an ascending order, the king, wise man, and prophet who correspond, according to Abulafia, to the aforementioned three created worlds. Abulafia continues:

> And there is no other nation which denies the greatness of our nation, law, language and script. All admit the efficacy of these four categories and also admit what derives from this, in other words, also thought, knowledge and acts. However, they say that was in the past and today it is not so, for there are other nations which have come closer to God than we are, and therefore, He has brought them closer to Himself. However, their admitting our greatness does not add or detract, for because we know the truth, what can we say when every one else admits it as well. . . . But the benefit here is for those who recognize the truth, and then turn from their deceit and return to the truth. And the damage is to those who continue to uphold it [their false faith] and do not make the effort to find the truth.[18]

Abulafia adopts a historical approach in that he posits that Christianity and (to a certain extent) Islam recognize their debt to Judaism as the source of their religions, and therefore, cannot deny the primacy of the Jews, though looking at current Jewish circumstances they can question whether this is still true today. However, Abulafia feels that once they have admitted that basic truth and applied the criteria outlined above, then there can be no doubts as to the conclusion reached. Here, the traditional Christian claim of Jewish stubbornness and blindness in not recognizing the truth is turned on its head, as it is now the members of the other faith who persist in living a lie, even though they know and necessarily admit the truth.[19]

Abulafia has a ready answer for those who claim that the Jews were once the chosen nation, but have now been superseded by others. He suggests that the greater the nation, the closer it was to God, the farther it had to fall if it was incapable of maintaining the standards needed for knowing the Divine truth. And therefore, it is not surprising that in this day and age, there is no other nation that has been and is so greatly humbled and oppressed. Though contemporary Jews do not act as they should, the potential is always there, as the Torah, the language, and the script that can lead them back to their previous greatness and knowledge of the truth have not been changed or replaced. Abulafia continues:

> And if you will say that in what they expounded, Jesus and Muhammad had no other intention than to unify the Divine name, I will answer that you are correct, if you can show that their new teachings were an improvement, materially, spiritually and intellectually, on that which existed previously [Jewish unification of the name].[20] For both of them emerged from our nation, and their teachings distanced those who were close to God in all three categories. And it is well known that they were not fathers who guided their children in the ways of God, but they found nations full of misguided people (*shotim*) and they released them from their bonds and they [the misguided people], as if they had been redeemed from a prison, rejoiced in them. . . . Even so, there are those among them who are *perfecti* (*shalem*) and knowers of the truth, and recognising the truth makes them as one who wishes to be attached to our nation. And they are called the righteous of the nations and merit a portion in the world to come.

For Abulafia, it was evident that neither Jesus nor Muhammad had been able to improve on what had existed prior to their appearance on the historical stage. Neither materially, spiritually, nor intellectually had they contributed anything worthwhile. Indeed, Abulafia suggests that they misled people who knew no better, though he is quick to point out that there are those among the Christians and Muslims who are aware of the truth. Abulafia then turns his attention to the Jews:

> And know, that without prejudice, I will tell the truth even about my nation. And it is that anyone today who boasts and claims that he is a Jew (*yehudi*) from the seed of Judah, in other words, of those who admit (*modim*) the truth, and who say "More than anything else in the world it is sufficient for us to know the name [of God]"

> for this is the reason they were called *Yehudim*—in other words *YHV Dayam* meaning "it is enough that they should call [God] by this name" . . .—And those who brag about this do not walk in the path of Abraham, our forefather, and Moses, our Teacher. For both of the latter taught us that circumcision (*brit milah*) is the perfection of our existence in this world, and it is the covenant of the language (*brit ha-lashon*) which brings us to the world to come.[21] So in all humility, I explicitly am saying that the bragger is not from the seed of Abraham in perfection, for there is something foreign in his essence, or in the blood of his ancestors. And therefore, I can also say that he is not from the disciples of Moses in perfection. However, whoever desires to instruct himself in order to be like them [Abraham and Moses] should follow their teachings, and even if he is not from them [from their seed] he will be them![22]

Judaism is not what most people think it is. True Judaism is the knowledge of the Divine name, and that is self-evident from the etymology of the word *Yehudim*. The first three letters of the word are the letters that make up the Tetragrammaton and the last part with vowel changes means "enough" or "sufficient." In other words, to be a true Jew, it is sufficient to know the essence of the Divine name. While Abulafia is convinced that he has rationally shown that the Jewish people were those closest to God by nature of their law, language, and script, even Judaism has layers of accretion that have distanced it from the original clarity of vision that it had. The knowledge of the name has become submerged by the vicissitudes of time, thus the commandments have also lost their original meaning and purpose. Contemporary Jews, even those braggers who claim to know the name, are misled because they do not know the Divine name in its entirety as it has been revealed to Abraham Abulafia, who is from the seed of Abraham and is a true disciple of Moses. And even though the followers of Jesus and Muhammad have been led astray because at the time, they were incapable of knowing any better, they also have the potential, if they are prepared to recognize the truth about the origins of the Jewish nation, to attain true knowledge of God. The Jews have a natural advantage in that they were the chosen people, they speak and write the language in which God revealed himself, follow the Torah and therefore, have the greatest potential to return to that sublime state of knowledge. Yet at present, they too, are incapable of living up to that potential.

This economy of salvation, which because of the status of the human species as the supreme element of creation, is universally attainable, if, however, dependant on recognizing that the Jews are the chosen nation and their past knowledge of the Divine name and essence far exceeds any other, is also elaborated in another Abulafian work, *Or ha-Sechel* (Light of the Intellect). In this work, also written in late 1285, Abulafia seemingly develops a version of the famous three rings parable.[23] It comes in the context of a discussion about the value of the different languages that exist in the world, and Abulafia emphasizes that all languages enjoy the Divine efflux, and that God takes them from potentiality to actuality.[24] If all languages are of Divine origin in that they emerge from the Divine speech, is there any difference between them? Abulafia's reply is that the difference between the languages is like the difference between the nations and their scripts discussed above. The Jews who received the Torah are surely superior to other nations, and were closer to God as long as they adhered correctly to the true faith. However, the farther they have distanced themselves from that true primal faith, the farther they are from God. Abulafia continues:

> And it is famous among the nations that our nation was the first to receive the Torah from the mouth of the Mighty. No other nation denies this, and thus, there is no need to prove it. If so, they whose matters have been dealt with by He Who Influences All are superior to all others, and their language is superior to the other languages. And the proof of this is that He [God] spoke all that He said in their language, and in its script commanded to write all that would be written. Moreover, if we will say that it was written by Him [God] on the two tablets, whether we accept this in its simple manner or whether by its revealed and hidden meaning together, and even if one be true and the other false, behold it was written in the Holy Language which persists until this day.

And if a person will say, it is true, but see how the nation is unfit for that high level, and has been replaced by another nation, and has changed the laws and commandments and made them fewer, and the script has been changed [i.e., to Greek or Latin]. Behold, he who says this is himself, without wanting to do so, admitting to the high level of that people, its language and script. And after he has admitted the core of the matter, his question is relevant because of the three virtues that are today missing from the people . . . [25]

But we will admit that today the three virtues are missing but not because one has been changed for another. But it is like a person who had a marvelous pearl and wanted to leave it for his son. And while he was educating his son in the ways of the rich so that he would appreciate the true value of the pearl, so that the son should appreciate it as much as the father, the son angered his father. What did the father do? He did not want to give the pearl to any other person so that the son should not lose his inheritance if he appeased his father, so he threw it into a pit saying "if my son does not appease me I do not want him to inherit but if he does I do not want him to lose it. In the meantime it will remain hidden (*ganuz*) in the pit and if he appeases me I will remove it from the pit and give it to him."[26]

All the time he did not appease his father, his father's servants would continually anger the son each one claiming that the Master had given him the pearl, yet the son was not worried for he was not of great understanding. After a time the son was so angry that he begged pardon, his father forgave him, extracted the pearl from the pit and gave it to him. When the father's servants saw this they fell on their faces and they were ashamed of the lies they had told the son. They had to do a lot before he forgave them the anger they had caused him.

This is what has happened to us with those that say that the Name has replaced us with others, and that we can't reply (lit. we have no mouth with which to speak) all the time that we do not appease the Name for all we have sinned to Him. But on our return and when He returns our inheritance, those that embarrassed us will be embarrassed before us when they see that God has returned our inheritance, and what they shattered and received was only an image . . .

> And because today, we are still not at that level, that we expect to ascend to any day, the argument continues as to who has the pearl and the truth, we or our oppressors. Until there comes He who decides who will raise the pearl from the pit and give it to whom He desires, us or them. And then the truth will be known and the pearl returned to its rightful owners who are called God's sons.[27] And jealousy, argument and hatred will cease, and false thoughts will be stamped out of hearts, and each and every person will see every other person as if he, his friend and his friend's friend are he himself, like a man sees every limb in his body that each one is him, and every part of every limb together is him as well. And then "many will wander (*yeshotetu*) and knowledge will increase" (Dan 12:4), and one will not teach his companion saying "know God," because all will know the Name from the smallest to the biggest like water is to the sea, "for the earth will be full of the knowledge of God like water covers the sea" (Isaiah 11:9), and because this is so all admit that the chosen of all languages is the Holy Language . . . [28]

A careful analysis of this passage shows that while Abulafia felt no sympathy for the other religions, he was also not enamored by the Judaism of his day, which he felt to be lacking and therefore not worthy of possession of the pearl.[29] At the start, Abulafia establishes the superiority of the Hebrew language as the language of revelation, and the nation who received the revelation as being the son of the parable. While the father was teaching the son to value riches so that he would be truly appreciative of the pearl, that is, the true meaning of revelation, the son angered the father, and the father hid the pearl. Abulafia is referring here to the revelation at Sinai when the true meaning of the Torah was given via Moses to the people of Israel. However, the sin of the Golden Calf resulted in a more superficial reading and understanding of the Divine text. The son is not wise enough to realize that he lacks the pearl, that is, the true interpretation of scriptures, and therefore does not really understand how the servants can claim to be in possession of the pearl. However, the son himself does not have the pearl, the scriptures are flawed without their true meaning, which will only be fully revealed when the son appeases his father. When the son repents, the full glory of the pearl is revealed, that is, the true knowledge of the Divine name achieved through the deeper internal meaning of the Torah and the Commandments, which reveal the true essence and knowledge of God. Yet, crucially, the servants who kept angering the son, always were and remain part of the household. They were never totally excluded as, according to the parable, they had, for a time, an image of the truth, albeit bearing very little resemblance to it.[30] Realizing their mistake, they are forgiven by the son and not excluded from the truth. Nor, after admitting their lies and mistakes, are they inferior in any way. They share fully in the knowledge of God. The "knowers of God," the *Yehudim,* are not the members of any particular religion, but share in the universal redemption based on knowledge of the Name.

Abulafia clearly expects the pearl to be revealed in the immediate future, and it is not hard to guess who is supposed to play a major role in the unfolding of events. In addition, Abulafia does not see any significant difference between the members of the faiths or their languages at the end of time, and views contemporary Jews as not much better than the Gentiles in their comprehension of the true faith. Their only real advantage is in their being of the Jewish nation, knowing the Hebrew language and script. However, what becomes clear is that there is a progression to the true faith based on the knowledge of the Divine name which supersedes the Jewish religion as it is practiced today and will unify humanity.[31] This does not mean that there will be a new revelation at the end of time, just the achievement of perfect understanding, never yet realized, of the revelation at Sinai. This also seems to imply a return to a unified language, Hebrew, which is the only language in which the Divine name can be properly known and enunciated and prophecy achieved.[32] Abulafia's ideal was of universal redemption and perfection, regardless of the faith people belong to, in the knowledge of God through knowledge of the Holy Name.

Abulafia's understanding of the end of days should be seen within the context of his ongoing polemical dialogue with the Franciscan Joachimites whose teachings seem to have been part of the formation of so much of his thought. As Salimbene reveals in his chronicle, Gerard of Borgo San Donino was an aberration, and most Franciscans understood Joachim to be talking about a third period, that of the Holy Spirit, in terms of a more spiritual and fuller understanding of both Testaments, not the appearance of another, newer Testament. For Joachim, the New Testament proceeds from the Old as the coming of Jesus replaces the revelation of the first advent. The New Testament will persevere until the second coming and the end of history, as is made clear both in the *Liber concordia* and the *Liber figurarum*.[33] The third period represents a perfect spiritual understanding, which proceeds from both the Old and New Testaments. For Abulafia, there could never be a New Testament, there was and is only one Torah. However, since the Golden Calf episode, it had never been read as it should have been, its true inner meaning had been hidden from all mankind. Thus, the Jews had interpreted the Torah by means of the oral law, according to the level of understanding given them; the Jews, being those chosen to receive the revelation and the users of the Divine language are always closer to the truth than Christians or Muslims. However, the true spiritual knowledge of the Torah as the Divine names will only be fully revealed and lived after the redemption, when Gentiles and Jews will join together in the true knowledge of the Name.

1280—Rome Revisited

It was in a state of heightened apocalyptic expectation that Abulafia made his way to Rome. Though presumably not revealing the reason in late 1270, God had already hinted that he would have to go to Rome, and when the moment arrived, Abulafia was more than prepared. Following the remarkable vision in Sicily in 1276, Abulafia had known for certain that he was the expected Messiah, and he was surely aware that significant events would occur in Rome. Indeed, the purpose of his very carefully planned audience with the pope was startling: he was to announce the impending end of Christianity in the world, teach the knowledge of the true Divine name, and put into motion the events of the last days, which would see an ingathering of the nations in the knowledge of the Divine name.

Rome had a long pedigree in the Jewish understanding of the role of the Messiah. Earlier rabbinical tradition stated that the Messiah had been born on the day of the destruction of the second temple and was to be found among the poor and the lepers at the gates of Rome.[1] The *Book of Zerubabel,* a popular apocalyptical work which has its original roots in the first century and was later redacted a number of times, actually had the Messiah hidden away in a church in that city, and portrayed a cosmic battle between the Messiah and Armilus.[2] During the course of the Barcelona disputation in the summer of 1263, Nahmanides had informed Friar Paul, his protagonist, that the Messiah would have to go and seek an audience with the pope.[3] In addition, a passage in the Zohar, which may reflect Abulafia's visit to Rome, also depicts the Messiah confronting the pope and the destruction of Rome.[4] Thus, the idea that the messianic figure had to face the leading representative of the dominant faith (or power) in the same manner that Moses appeared before Pharaoh was widely known and accepted in Jewish circles in the second half of the thirteenth century.

From Abulafia's point of view, everything that had happened from the first vision in 1270 had been in preparation for this visit in Rome, which was planned very carefully down to the exact day and moment that he was to meet with the pope. This event had cosmic as well as historical significance, and came at the moment when Abulafia assumed that he would don his public mantle of messiahship. The sources for this visit to Rome and its ultimate purpose survive in a very problematic format. Abulafia recounts that in the buildup to the visit, he wrote a number of prophetic books, none of which are extant. However, in the aftermath of the visit, and perhaps as a result of it, he wrote commentaries on these prophetic works. What is strange about the commentaries is that they are written in reverse order, in other words, he comments on the last prophetic book first and works his way through them back to the first one. Additionally strange is that he tries to hide his identity as commentator, referring to himself as the "Little Abubrahim"[5] and as the disciple of Raziel "my master" these thirteen years. This Abubrahim receives a vision in which he understands that he is to write the commentaries to the prophetic works. Raziel is numerically equal to Abraham (248) and is one of the ways Abulafia refers to himself in various works.[6] In addition, Raziel is also an important angel who reveals the secrets of the Lord. Thus, Abulafia identifies himself with Raziel, as he is revealing the Divine secrets, yet here, he seems to take on another identity in order to be able to comment on the prophetic books and the secrets they contain.

The commentaries are often cryptic and difficult to decipher and they contain phrases and sections from the original prophetic works, which are then explained. The commentaries were probably written in 1282–1283, as the "thirteen years" mentioned above probably refers back to the first vision of 1270. The book was definitely completed before 1285.[7] There were six prophetic books and a seventh book that Abulafia refers to as "half a book," which is the most important part of the whole work and which appears last, as its name—*Sefer ha-Haftarah* (The Additional Book)—indicates, referring to the additional reading from the prophets that accompanies the reading of the Torah scroll in the synagogue on Saturdays and Festivals. The whole work is given the name *Metzaref ha-Sechel* (Furnace of the Mind), which, Abubrahim mentions, is numerically equivalent to *Mishkan ha-Sechel* (Sanctuary of the Mind), which is its internal or esoteric secret. This follows the Abulafian method that links external events with internal processes as the macrocosm and the microcosm come together. The commentaries deal with both actual historical occurrences and their cosmic and internal repercussions and significance.

The text dealing with the visit to Rome appears in the commentary to *Sefer ha-Edut,* the Book of Testimony, which was the fourth of the prophetic books to be written. The prophecy itself was given in Rome just before Abulafia's attempt to see the pope, as a testimony or witness to the fact that he was prepared to become a martyr for the cause. The commentary is very important because it also contains the details of a number of visions that Abulafia had in Rome in the month leading up to the appointed date for the papal audience. These visions, along with others that appear in the other commentaries, give a pretty clear indication of how Abulafia perceived himself and what he intended to say during the audience. The visions all deal with the true knowledge of the Tetragrammaton and its renewal, given that, according to Abulafia, since the days of primal man its true essence had been concealed. The purpose of the revelation at this particular moment is because the end of days is close, and Abulafia, born in the year this all-powerful Divine name was renewed and crowned over all others, is the one chosen to make the name known to all mankind.[8]

It is from true knowledge of the Divine name in all its combinations that the path toward redemption is uncovered, and the significance of the actual date of the papal audience is derived. For the date of the meeting is tied in with the true meaning of the famous verse from Daniel 7:25, "He shall speak words against the Most High, and shall wear out the saints of the Most High, and shall think to change the times and the law, and they shall be given into his hands for a time, two times and half a time."[9] According to Abulafia, the latter section of the verse contains within itself two Divine names: *Adonai* (65) and the Tetragrammaton (26). For if the word *time* signifies the Tetragrammaton, then "two times and half a time" is equal to *Adonai* (26 x 2.5). Thus, inherent in this famous verse from Daniel is the time that the true name with its correct enunciation will be revealed and there will be no need to use *Adonai* anymore.[10]

When the Hebrew word for truth *emet,* is applied to this verse, it is the key that opens the door to understanding how and when the redemption will come about.[11] *Emet* when read as a number is 1440 which Abulafia understands to imply the passing of a "time" in its historical context. When calculated, "a time, two times and half a time" [1440 + (2 x 1440) + 720] would therefore work out to be the year 5040 AM, in other words 1280 AD. In addition, Abulafia writes that the year 5040 is also the one when the sun will "emerge from potentiality (*koah* = 28) to actuality (*poal* = 180), in other words, that is when 180 cycles of 28 are completed." The power of the sun, which has had potentiality for one hundred and eighty cycles of twenty-eight years, will, by becoming actuality, wane in 1280 AD.[12] The sun is clearly a reference to Christianity, its calendar year a solar one, and the continuation of the passage indicates that Abulafia is really referring to the end of its dominion: "And when ten years are added, behold the complete number will be the All (*ha-kol*—5050) in the secret of *yud* (10) . . . and it is the end (*ha-Sof*) of the world *peh-vav* (86) *samech-heh* (65), and 5050 years will be completed.[13] And it is what he revealed to us in hinting at the revelations in which was revealed to him the wonderful end (*ketz* = 190). For behold *kuf-peh* (180) cycles and another 10 years equals 'ketz' and it is the secret of 'the day of vengeance' (*nakam* = 190). And the hint 'for the day of vengeance is in my heart, the year of my redemption cometh (*geuli ba'ah* = 5050)' (Isa. 63:4)."[14] The Hebrew word for end, *ketz,* signals that another ten years will pass after the waning of the power of the sun before the end will finally come, and these ten years are needed in order to complete the All (*ha-kol*), which as a number reads 5050 AM, in other words 1290 AD.[15] In addition, Abulafia hints at the end of the reign of two of the Divine names which are numerically equal to the word *the end, Elohim* (86) and *Adonai* (65), which are the exilic names of God. There is a direct reference to this by the prophet Isaiah who refers to the day of vengeance that will occur in the year of redemption, which again indicates that the end and vengeance (190) will occur in 1290.[16]

These convoluted calculations, which appear a number of other times in Abulafia's later works in various forms, indicate the importance of both the years 1280 and 1290. In a work written in 1289, a commentary on *Sefer Yetzirah,* which contains a number of references to Christianity and Jesus, Abulafia shows that the Hebrew word for truth (*emet*) also reveals the true year of the final redemption, even according to the Christian calendar. In this work, the end of the reign of the sun and its power over Israel in the year 1280 is made far more explicitly, and its connection to Christianity is also emphasized in that the name of Jesus (spelled as it might have been pronounced in southern Europe—*het, zayin, vav, zayin*) has the numerical value of twenty-eight, the same as *koah*—potential. Hence, the potential of Christianity ends as the 180 cycles comes to a close, and here Abulafia refers to the next ten years as a transition period in which the power of Christianity wanes leading up to the end in 1290.[17] Abulafia takes the word from Genesis 2:4 "This is the story of the heavens and earth when they were created—*behibaram*" (which also just happens to include the letters of his own name Abraham) and dissects the word into two parts—*bet heh* and *aleph bet resh mem.* The first two letters indicate the ratio between the numerical value of the Tetragrammaton (26), and the way that it is commonly pronounced (*adonai*—65), that is, a ratio of 5:2 which when put into Hebrew words—*hamisha* (5) and *shnaiim* (2) numerically equals the Hebrew for "fifty years" referring to the verse from Lev 25:10, "and thou shall sanctify the fiftieth year." The second part of the word when the last letter (*mem* = 40) is numerically broken down farther (into *kaph* = 20 and *dalet, yud, vav* = 20), then reads *abarech dayo,* and if the first part of this is read as a number, it then means that 1222 years are enough of exile. Given that according to rabbinic tradition, the destruction of the temple took place in 68 AD, the word *be-hibaram* when correctly understood refers to the year 1290, the fiftieth year of the sixth millennium, and to the central place of the Divine names in the process of redemption. However, the Hebrew word for "truth" (*emet*) also reveals the exact year of the end, as according to Abulafia, it was the letters that make up this word (*aleph mem tav*) that appeared to Daniel (7:1) in his dream. Read as an abbreviation, these letters make up the words **E***leph* **M***a'ataim* **T***ishi'im*—one thousand two hundred and ninety, which, says Abulafia, is the corresponding year in the Christian calendar to the year 5050 in the Jewish.[18]

Thus, the significance of the year 1280 AD for the papal audience derives from an understanding of Christianity, which gives it an essential role on both the cosmic level and in history, and points to a particular moment that heralds momentous change. It is impossible to ignore Christianity, and the politics of salvation and redemption intimately connect Jews and Christians. Hence, it is imperative to have knowledge of Christianity, its founder, and its role in the progression of history. Abulafia reverses the traditional Christian opinion of Judaism in that the former becomes the carnal religion, while the latter, notwithstanding its current problematical status, is spiritual. This is because Judaism was the closest reflection of the Divine revelation and could never be superseded by anything else, whereas, at best, Christianity was a pale image and a total misunderstanding of the Torah. Abulafia, reading the Torah according to the keys given him by the Active Intellect, was able to incorporate Jesus into the text, and through the use of gematria, letter combination, and other hermeneutical devices, show the negative aspects of his personality and religious claims.[19] In other words, like the proliferation of nations and languages that came about as a result of human nature as shown in the interpretation of the Tower of Babel episode, the other religions and religious leaders also have a historical role within the Divine economy, and therefore, must be represented in the Torah.[20] Therefore, it is not surprising to find that while Abulafia's attitude toward Christianity and its founder is extremely negative, its power, symbols, sacraments, liturgy, and significance are not dismissed out of hand, and have even to be read into the biblical text.

This prefiguration is found in Genesis 3:1 with regard to the serpent who tempted Eve to eat the fruit of the Tree of Knowledge leading to the expulsion from the Garden of Eden. Abulafia cites the verse "*ha-nahash haya 'arum* (the serpent was cunning)" and comments that "*ha-nahash* (363) is numerically equal to *ha-mashiah* (363)—the messiah, and *'arum*—cunning is numerically equal to *Yeshu*—Jesus [both are 316]." In addition, when the letters that make up the word *arum* are spelled out in full (*'ayin, resh, vav, mem*)[21] they become an anagram of *arum min yeshu* meaning that the cunning of the snake comes from Jesus. This implies that the serpent who misleads Eve, prefigures the false messiah Jesus who is cunning and who will mislead mankind, and because he "was both cunning and a magician, it [meaning both the serpent and Jesus] was cursed."[22] This prefiguration is also found in the story of the exodus from Egypt, particularly in the character of Pharaoh who presented himself as the highest God of Egypt and as the ruler of the whole world, and the first of all created beings. Abulafia's portrayal of the Egyptian king based on his interpretation of key biblical verses, allows him to see in Pharaoh the image of Jesus about whom the Christians falsely claim that he is both God and man.[23]

Abulafia shows that Pharaoh is numerically equivalent to Ashmadai (355), a common name for Satan, and that he is also the Teli (Draco), the mythical dragon or beast, mentioned in *Sefer Yetzirah* "who is like a king on his throne in this universe," is the attribute of judgment, and wields impure power.[24] The Teli is a beast with the power of sorcery, which according to Abulafia derives its supremacy from the seventy-two letter name of God when it is read in groups of three letters, set out in twelve columns, with six names to a row, implying eighteen letters in each line. This is connected with verses from Job (3:19) and Numbers (21:8–9), where it says regarding the copper serpent: "and all who were bitten and looked at the copper serpent (*nahash*), saw it, and lived (*ve-hai*)." *Vav, Yud,* and *Het,* which spell the word meaning "and lived," are numerically six (*vav*) and eighteen (*yud, het*), hence the order, but the numerical value of *nahash* is equal to "the name eighteen" (*shem yud het* = 358), and eighteen also stands for the number of years it takes the Teli / *nahash* to complete its heavenly cycle, and the number of months in every cycle that the Teli is to be found in each of the star signs it controls. According to Abulafia, in the crucial year 5040 (1280 AD), the Teli completed 280 cycles (280 x 18).[25]

Jesus was born from the tail of the Teli which is vanquished in the tenth plague by the power of the name used by Moses, the first redeemer.[26] The verse in Exodus 12 in which God reveals to Moses that He will go through Egypt killing the firstborns in the middle of the night (*ke-hatzot ha-laylah*), really refers to the victory over the Teli or the darkening of its power in that the letters of *ke-hatzot ha-laylah* when rearranged read *hatzel koah ha-teli*—shadow or curb the power of the Teli. Shadow refers to darkness (*ha-hoshech*), which when its letters are rearranged reads "the power of the lamb" (*koah ha-seh*), implying that the sacrifice of the paschal lamb on that night defeats the Teli allowing for the redemption to take place.[27] Thus, the redemption takes place both on the cosmic level as the false gods of Egypt and their sorcery along with Pharaoh are defeated, and on the historical level with the exodus from Egypt as a result of the tenth plague. This is also what will happen to Jesus, who is a false god in the same way Pharaoh was, and though his power is real as it derives from the Teli, it cannot match the knowledge of the true Divine name.[28]

Referring to the section in the Torah that deals with those who bear false witness (Deut. 19:15–21), Abulafia shows that the severe punishment meted out to those guilty of this most serious of offenses is due also to both Jesus and his mother, Mary (*Yeshu ve-Miriam*) whose names are numerically equal to "the alien gods of the lands (*elohei nehar ha-aretz* = 612)." *Ve-hanisharim*—the remnant—the first word of verse 20, is an anagram spelling out the names of Jesus and Mary, and as the verse continues, "they will hear and be afraid, and they will not continue to do anymore this evil thing [bearing false witness] in your midst."[29] In other words, when the Messiah reveals the truth, the false premises of Christianity and its central figures will become clear to all. And this, says Abulafia, is a hint of the seal dependent on time and which will end with *Va-yechulu*. The latter is the first word of the paragraph in Genesis 2 dealing with the seventh day, the Sabbath. Abulafia continues: "And the seal of *Yom Ha-Shishi* (the sixth day) is *Yeshua Ha-Notzri* (Jesus the Nazarite), but the seal of *Yom Ha-Shevii* (the seventh day) which is half the Name is the potential of the *Melech ha-Mashiah* (the King Messiah). . . ."[30] The first letters of both "the sixth day" and "Jesus the Nazerite" are *Yud Heh* (also the first two letters of the Tetragrammaton) and both terms are numerically equal (671), implying that Jesus' power is strongest on that particular day, the day of the crucifixion. While the first letters of "the seventh day" are also the first two letters of the Tetragrammaton, it is, however, numerically equal with the power of "the King Messiah" (both 453) who will vanquish the false pretender.

This idea is first found in a work written in 1280, probably in the aftermath of the visit to Rome, as again there is reference to that year symbolizing the end of the reign of the sun in the manner referred to above, and a rather cryptic connection between matter (carnality) and Christianity.[31] In addition, the book spells out in great detail the techniques that need to be followed in order to achieve knowledge of the Divine name and refers to the renewed name the Messiah is to reveal. Here, there is a correlation between the sixth day and the first two letters of the Tetragrammaton (*yud heh*), and the seventh day and the King Messiah and the last two letters (*vav heh*): "And even though half the name is like the whole name, behold the half of the name which reveals the secret of the King Messiah, and its secret the seventh day, rules over 'the body of Satan (*guf ha-Satan*)' whose name is Tammuz."[32] While there is no explicit mention here of Jesus, and though the numerical value of all three terms, King Messiah, the body of Satan, and Tammuz, are the same (453), the latter two are ruled over by the former, indicating that they are connected with the first half of the Tetragrammaton, as is Jesus, and with the sixth day. Abulafia mentions that Tammuz is the name for an ancient type of idolatry particularly attractive to women, and it is plausible to assume that the body of Satan refers to Jesus as the founder of a material religion, Christianity. This is also an indicator as to what day of the week Abulafia intended to arrange his papal audience, as it is clear that the King Messiah had to defeat the false messiah on his most powerful day—Friday.[33]

That Jesus is the founder of a material or carnal religion, while Abulafia is the true Messiah and representative of the spiritual faith becomes apparent in the continuation of the Torah commentary. Abulafia plays on a well-known Christian tradition that Jesus was crucified on wood from the Tree of Knowledge writing:

> [A]nd this same thing will happen sometime in the next two years (*mi-can ve-ad shenatayim*) in the matter of the Messiah with Jesus, for this is the reason that for the Greek Christians, the messiah is called *Anti Christus,* in other words the Master of that man, hinted in the verse "that man, the master of the land spoke harshly with us" (Gen. 42:30). And the issue is that he [the Messiah] will stand up to him and will inform everyone that what he [Jesus] said to the Christians that he is a God, the son of God and a man was a total fabrication. For he did not receive any power from the Special Name, but all his strength is dependent on the image of the *Teli* which is crucified (*talui*) on the Tree of Good and Evil Knowledge. And the Messiah is crucified on the Tree of Life which is the foundation upon which everything depends. And Jesus had a physical crucifixion because he crucified himself on a physical tree. And the Messiah is crucified these eighteen years on a spiritual thing, which is the Divine Intellect, and there remains two years of the period of his crucifixion.[34]

Abulafia plays on the meaning of Greek and Latin terms, spelling them out in Hebrew letters in order to tease out from within them their secret and true meanings. Abulafia, who is clearly the Messiah of the passage, refers to himself as the true Antichrist in that the real meaning of the term is Master of the Christ, when the Latin word, *anti* or as he reads or pronounces it, *adni,* is spelled in Hebrew (*aleph, daled, nun, yud*). In other words, Abulafia focuses on the Christian expectation of the coming of the Antichrist in the immediate future, but reveals that the supposedly greatest enemy of Christ and Christianity is really the Master of Christ.[35] The teachings of Jesus are patently false because the source of his power is the Teli which was crucified on the Tree of Knowledge in the heavens while he was crucified on a physical tree below. However, the true Messiah, Abulafia, has been crucified for these past eighteen years, in other words, since 1270, on the Tree of Life, "which is the foundation of all and the Divine Intellect" and will be revealed in all his glory in the next two years.[36]

Abulafia also denigrates the Christian liturgy and sacraments, particularly the central elements of the Eucharist, which he also finds mentioned in the Torah.[37] He carefully analyzes Joseph's interpretation of the dreams of Pharaoh's cup bearer and baker while they were in prison with him as recounted in Genesis 40, and shows that the dreams reveal the dependence of Christian sacraments on the power of demons. In the first instance, the baker who was crucified (*talui*) had three baskets on his head with bread and other delicacies loved by Pharaoh, and these were being pecked at by birds: "This hints at what Jesus said about the bread, which is for them [the Christians] the *corpus daemons,* which are the bodies [*sic*] of demons, the opposite of *domines* which is truly spiritual and Godly, according to their lies." Again, turning Abulafia's shaky Latin into Hebrew reveals that the Christians eat the bodies of demons, not the body of God, which the birds could never have pecked, when celebrating the Eucharist. In addition, *daemons* is also numerically equivalent (and made up of the same letters) to *dimyon*—imagination, again emphasizing the lesser status of Christianity as a religion of the imagination, not the intellect, and of the satanic realm.[38] The dream of the cup bearer, whose name reveals numerically that he is the Chief of Magicians, also demonstrates the physical and demonic nature of Christianity, as the vines (*ha-sarigim* = 558) hide within them the demon of magic (*sar magia* = 558). Thus, the Christian claim for the transubstantiation of the wine in the Eucharist is false as it is the work of the demons not God.

Almost every element of the two dreams gets similar treatment to show the carnal, magical, and demonic aspects of Christianity and its sacraments.[39] In the midst of this deconstruction of the dreams, Abulafia writes: "And for all of that, these fools thought that these powers were Divine and they make *sacrificio* from the bread desiring [it to be] flesh and its secret is *sheker officio,* in other words a false office." Again, the Latin word when spelt in Hebrew reveals the true nature of the office as a false one. This also leads Abulafia to the Latin term *sacremento* which becomes *sheker mento,* or a lying error (based on the Latin *mendo*), in other words, Christians swear in vain, and also the Latin *secreto* which when spelled out in Hebrew *shekertu* means "you are lying" (*sheker tu*), and when the order of the letters are changed slightly spells *christo:* "and behold it is saying to him [to Jesus] you are lying, for three (*shelosha* = 635) in gematria is 'lie and falsehood' (*sheker ve-kazav* = 635), anyone who thinks about the Name that it divides into two or three or more persona, he is an idol worshipper and a heretic."[40] Again, the Hebrew language, revealing all truth, conclusively demonstrates the inherent falsehood of Christianity and its central dogmas.

Though a false religion based on deception from the outset, Christianity, because it derives its power from the Teli, which controls the destiny of the world, has an important role in the process of redemption. The intimate link between the cosmic, the world-stage and the inner being of the individual, also dictated when and how events would unfold. Everything pointed to the end of the Jewish year 5040 as being the time when the power of the Teli, the sun, and Christianity would wane.[41] The day of the audience was to be a Friday, so that the power of the Tetragrammaton would be revealed in all its glory, defeating the Teli / Christ and his representative here on earth on their most influential day.

It now remains to see what happened on the way to Rome and in the buildup to the audience itself, and this is best told by Abulafia himself:

> This *Book of Testimony* is the fourth book of the commentary of Raziel [Abraham] that is the third to be written. For the *Sefer ha-Yashar* was the first written by Raziel and it was in the town of Patras in Greece. He wrote it in the year 5039 of the Creation (1279) when he

was 39 years old, in the ninth year from the start of his prophecies. But until that year he had not written any book that could be attributed to prophecy unless you were to count the many other books of wisdom and among them the books of the secret Kabbalistic lore that he had written. And, in that ninth year, the Name told him to go to Rome as he had commanded him in Barcelona in the year *ha-El* (5031 AM, late 1270 AD). On his way, he passed through Trani and was apprehended by strangers (*zarim*) having been informed on by Jews, and a miracle occurred and the Name removed and saved him from there. He passed through Capua and wrote there in the tenth year after leaving Barcelona, a second book, *Sefer ha-Haim.* And in the fifth month from Nissan which is the eleventh month from Tishri and is the month of Ab in the tenth year (1280), he came to Rome and intended to go on the day before *Rosh ha-Shana* (the Jewish New Year) before the Pope. And the Pope commanded all his gatemen, as he was then in Soriano, a town one day's distance from Rome, that if Raziel was to come there to talk to him in the name of all "yahadut" (*be-shem yahadut clal*) that he should immediately be stopped and denied entry. But he should be taken out of the town, and burned, and the wood is just outside the inner gate of the town. And this was all told to Raziel but he paid no heed to their words, but secluded himself and saw visions and wrote them down and he renewed this book, called the *Sefer ha-Edut,* to be a witness between him and the Name, that he gave up his life for the love of His commandments. And that it should also be a witness that He [the Name] saved him from his enemies, because on the day of his going before the Pope he became a two edged [sword] (*noldu lo shtei piyot*),[42] and when he entered the outer gates of the town a messenger came out to him and informed him that the night before the one seeking to kill him had suddenly died of a plague, suddenly in the night was struck [based on Daniel 5:30] and died, and Raziel was saved. And he was detained (*nitpas*) in Rome by the Little Brothers (Franciscans) and he stayed with them for 28 days,[43] for on the Fast of Gedalya he was detained in the year *haele* it is the year 5041 and he left on the first day of the month of Marḥeshvan.[44]

Perhaps unsurprisingly, according to Abulafia's version of events, the road to Rome was not smooth. He would have made no secret of his intended purpose, and given the very precarious situation of the Jewish communities of southern Italy, it is not surprising that they attempted to hinder his progress. Trani had a sizeable Jewish community which was being targeted by the Dominicans, and Abulafia's arrest, presumably at the instigation of the community, was probably an act of self-preservation. However, a miracle occurred, quite possibly in the shape of Franciscan Joachimites who may have intervened on his behalf, allowing Abulafia to continue to Rome.[45] His testimony reveals that he arrived in Rome in good time, giving himself at least a month to get everything arranged for the audience. According to the text, he intended to have the audience on the eve of the Jewish New Year, yet this should not be taken to mean literally on the eve, as from the continuation it becomes evident that as Abulafia approached the papal residence in Soriano, he was informed that the pope had died. Nicholas III died suddenly on Thursday evening, August 22, 1280, and the Jewish New Year was set to begin on the next Monday night, August 26. The Jewish day starts at nightfall and therefore, as far as Abulafia was concerned, the pope died on "*yom ha-shishi,*" the sixth day of the week, Friday.[46] It was crucial that Abulafia see the pope on the Friday, and this was the last one before the end of the Jewish year 5040, when all the indicators pointed at the waning of the power of Christianity. The fact that the pope did not want to see him, and indeed threatened him with death had not deterred Abulafia who was prepared to sacrifice his own life, and the pope's death was a clear vindication of his revelations, and his own role in the unfolding of events. The metaphorical two-edged sword that was given to Abulafia, a reflection of the real sword with which Ehud ben Gera killed the Moabite king, Eglon, had given the pope his comeuppance.[47] The power of Christianity was indeed on the wane, and Abulafia's predictions had come true.[48]

It is also clear from this text and the rest of the prophetic commentaries what Abulafia had intended to say to the pope if he had been granted his audience.[49] He had come to speak "in the name of all *Yahadut,*" which, in this context, does not mean Judaism. The word *yahadut* was used in the Middle Ages to express the spiritual qualities of Judaism, not as a proper noun meaning the Jewish people, and for Abulafia the etymology of *yahadut* was *hodayah*—knowing or recognizing the truth.[50] Truth is knowledge of the Divine name which is central to Abulafia's understanding of redemption and indeed central to the whole system of Abulafian Kabbalah.[51] For Abulafia, the proper noun *yehudim* (Jews) actually means *yud heh vav* (the letters of the Tetragrammaton) *dayam* meaning that the true Jew is one who admits (*meha-modim be-emet*) that knowledge of the four-lettered Divine name is enough and superior to everything else.[52] In other words, Abulafia's intention was to inform the pope about the power of the Divine name, and this becomes clear from the content of the visions that Abulafia has and which are recorded in the continuation of *Sefer ha-Edut:*

> And know, that most of the visions that Raziel saw where all structured around the knowledge and renewed revelation of the Divine name (*shem ha-meforash*) now in the world, in these days, and it has not been like this from Adam till now, and it is the root of all his books. . . . And he first wrote all this in another book he wrote which he called *Get ha-Shemot,* and he intended in it to reveal to every man of intellect that the (Divine) names are the rulers in the world and they are all attributed to the essence of the Primal Cause. But they [the Divine names] are like nothing in comparison with the kingship of the four lettered Hidden Name which is the King of all Kings, and by it alone that the Lord wishes to be known. And the Lord crowned It [the Hidden Name] in the year 5000 (late 1239–1240) and it is the year that Abraham was born. . . . And therefore, Raziel denied kingship to all the other attributed names, and crowned this name alone.[53]

Here, Abulafia establishes a connection between the year of his birth, the renewed revelation of the four-lettered Hidden Name which is superior to all the other Divine names, and implied here is that this is the essence of his mission. Abulafia's purpose was to teach Christianity the true name in its fullness, and bring about the redemption. He also emphasizes his own messianic status in this commentary and states emphatically that the Messiah, who has been anointed king and is the redeemer, "and he is I and I am he," is a *yehudi* who will come to reveal a new faith, which is the knowledge of the Divine Name. And it is this knowledge of the name, newly revealed, that seals the end of the exile, even though the children of Israel themselves are still mostly ignorant about it.[54]

According to the commentary on *Sefer ha-Haim,* while in Capua Abulafia wrote a work called *Hotam ha-Haftarah* (Seal of the Addition), which he considered to be the most important of all his compositions.[55] According to the introduction, when he left Capua to go to Rome, Abulafia took "this very distinguished book," which focuses on the knowledge of the Divine names and his messianic status, with him.[56] The true esoteric name of *Hotam ha-Haftarah* is the "Book of the Gospel (*Sefer ha-Besorah* = 858) whose secret is the Rainbow of Noah (*keshet Noah* = 858), and therefore, he called it Sanctifiable Holiness (*kedoshim kadishim* = 858) because he enumerated new and wonderful statutes (*shat hukim* = 858), in other words, the ineffable Name (*Shem ha-Meforash*), the foundation of all the books."[57] This series of expressions with equal numerical value indicate that this book, the real Gospel with the secrets of the Divine name, was taken to Rome to be taught to the pope. In the work, Abulafia is described as one who has the holy spirit within him, and as the highest of all mountains sent out to fight against all those who have forgotten the Divine name. And in the continuation: "Release release those who think [*hoshvei shemo*—calculate, try to discover; based on Malachi 3:16] on His name, for I am renewing a new Torah amidst the holy nation, who are my people Israel, my honourable Name is in a new Torah, and it has not been pronounced by my people since the day I hid my countenance from them, and if it is the hidden name, it is pronounceable. And then He commanded him [Abulafia] to not hide His name any more from the true seekers and He revealed it to him in all its sanctity . . ."[58]

In addition, the title of the first of the prophetic books, *Sefer ha-Yashar,* perhaps is a reference to the book mentioned in the Bible which in the Midrash becomes a work of such length that the whole Torah is but one line of it.[59] It is a book that connects Elijah with the Messiah; Elijah reads from the book and the enemies of Israel are destroyed, allowing the Messiah to take all the spoils.[60] Another of the prophetic books is named *Sefer ha-Brit ha-Hadashah* (Book of the New Gospel), which deals with the combination of letters of one verse, which Abulafia himself constructs and which includes the words, "YHWH will reign for ever, and He made a new covenant (*brit hadashah*) with his people, and His Name will be believed."[61] Thus, Abulafia seems to be suggesting that he, as Messiah, is revealing a new Torah that is based on the knowledge of the Tetragrammaton.[62] While different from Gerard of Borgo San Donnino's *Introductorius in evangelium eternum* in that the latter suggested that Joachim's works were a new revelation, there is a clear relationship with the Joachite idea of a new spiritual understanding of the Old and New Testaments for the new age. Armed with *Hotam ha-Haftarah,* a new gospel, Abulafia, as Messiah, intended to reveal to the Pope the redemptive power of the Tetragrammaton, and usher in the ten-year period that would signal the waning of Christianity, and make known the true essence of *Yahadut.*[63]

In the immediate aftermath of the visit to Rome, Abulafia, now in Messina, wrote the last of his prophetic works, *Sefer ha-Melitz.*[64] From the commentary to this work written in 1283, it seems that a euphoric Abulafia felt that he had achieved his goals on all levels. The expedition to Rome was the outward actual manifestation of a parallel internal path, both of which climaxed at the same time. Abulafia explains that the term Messiah refers to three things—the Active Intellect, the actual Messiah who will bring about the redemption with the aid of the power of the Active Intellect, and the human intellect, which works to redeem a person from all material desires.[65] The physical journey to Rome was mirrored by an internal one, which was the battle to free himself from the power of the "Great King," Satan, the imagination, which misleads one to concentrating on material things rather than spiritual. Abulafia's goal was to crown the "Small King," the intellect, and by doing so, cleave to the Active Intellect. As Abulafia progressed along the path, he received aid from God who sent angels who gave him new names and helped him proceed until he was appointed messenger to reveal the Divine truth. This internal struggle is a reflection of his activities as Messiah, as the trials and tribulations leading to his victory over the pope, the "Great King," and the waning of the power of Christianity symbolizes the victory of the "Small King," the Messiah who is aided by the Active Intellect. The inner and outer redemptions joined together and culminated in Rome where on the "eve of the Jewish New Year," the "Great King" was finally overcome and the "Small King" emerged victorious.[66]

Thus, Abulafia's putative charisma, which he claimed was divinely inspired had led him, against all odds, to Rome where, according to him, he was to meet with Christ's vicar on earth on that portentous Friday, in late August 1280. From Abulafia's point of view, the purpose of the meeting was crystal clear. He was the appointed Messiah sent to announce the impending end of the power of Christ in this world, and the ushering in of a new age, the foundation of which was based on true knowledge of the Divine name. Nicholas III's refusal to grant him an audience was of no real consequence as the whole process was preordained, and the pope's sudden death was clear indication of this. The election of another pope half a year later would not matter as it would represent the desperate attempt of a dying institution to hold on to its days of glory. For Abulafia, the wheels of the final redemption had been set into motion and 1290 would be his vindication.

Abulafia the "Diplomat": Was There Method in his Madness?

In 1524, a Jewish princely pretender made his way to Rome to seek an audience with Pope Clement VII. David ha-Reuveni claimed that he was the brother of King Joseph from the tribe of Reuben who lived in the Desert of Habor (based on II Kings 16:6; I Chronicles 5:26), who had a powerful army and wished to join forces with the Christians to combat the Turks. A Jewish portrait painter, Moses da Castellazzo arranged for David to go to Rome and be introduced to Cardinal Giles of Viturbo who arranged for an audience with Clement VII. The audience took place and David received letters of introduction to the King of Portugal, and the story continues until its sad end with his execution in 1538.[1] Giles of Viturbo, a leading humanist and Cabbalist, was certain that the end of days were nigh and that David ha-Reubeni and Solomon Molcho, who followed him, were part of the fulfillment of prophecies dealing with the eschaton.[2] This was the reason he supported them both and arranged for papal audiences. Thus, it was possible for Jews with messianic pretensions and with the right connections to obtain papal audiences. Though more than two hundred years earlier, and in an entirely different historical context, is it possible to uncover similar circumstances that would have gained Abulafia entry into the papal presence?

There were two possible networks that Abulafia could have utilized in order to gain a papal audience. The first was among his Jewish contemporaries in the Iberian Peninsula, Rome, and its environs, particularly those teaching and writing commentaries on Maimonides' *Guide for the Perplexed*. The second network, and one more difficult to identify is the Franciscan-Joachimite. Here matters are more complex given the dearth of sources for Franciscan houses in Rome in the mid-to-late thirteenth century and also because being a Joachimite does not mean that one was necessarily a spiritual, nor does it mean that there were no relations with others in the order who did not embrace the teachings of Joachim. These two very different networks have one possible interconnection in the person of Maestro Gaio, a Jew who was doctor to cardinals and popes.

It is crucial to remember that the only evidence for what occurred in Rome is Abulafia's account. There are no extant documents from papal or other sources that give an indication that Abulafia's activities in Rome made any impression whatsoever. Thus, everything that happened in Rome is described from his perspective and from how he perceived things. This, naturally, gives rise to the suspicion that it was hyperbole, or the product of a megalomaniac with little connection to reality. Yet, looking at the account in *Sefer ha-Edut,* translated in the previous chapter, and the way it evolves, there are good reasons to suppose that even if totally subjective, it contains grains of truth. For instance, what was the purpose in mentioning that he spent almost a month with the Franciscans if he did not? And why choose the Franciscan Order, and not any other branch of the Church, if they did not hold particular significance for him? Given that the Franciscan-Joachimite context is so important for understanding Abulafia's teachings, it stands to reason that he mentioned the Franciscans and this climactic end to the stay in Rome because it indeed happened.

Looking more closely at what Abulafia writes about the twenty-eight days he spent with the Franciscans in Rome after his attempt to see the pope, suggests that he was helped by elements in the order. However, the question then has to be asked: Why would the Franciscans want to help someone who was so incredibly negative about Christ and the Virgin Mary, who denigrated the sacraments, who was preaching about the approaching end of Christianity, and who, even for a friar with grievances against the Church, was spouting pure blasphemy? Abulafia was not backward about his desire to convert his Christian interlocutors, including the pope, to his version of Judaism, so what would have motivated them to aid Abulafia in his attempt to meet with Nicholas III? It is also clear from his works and the account in *Sefer ha-Edut* that he was not a diplomat, in the sense that he kept his true opinions under wrap and did not reveal all his aces before the anticipated interview. His arrest in Trani, surely an attempt at damage limitation by the Jewish community, must be an indication of his total lack of reticence.

While based on speculation, it is reasonable to assume that the Franciscan reaction to Abulafia was not homogeneous. For those attracted to the teachings of Joachim, Abulafia's announcement that he was the Antichrist (based on his interpretation of the term), while inspiring fear and dread, might have been seen as part and parcel of events leading up to the end of second status, expected in 1290. Though the Franciscans might not have believed that he was actually the Antichrist, tradition held that the Antichrist would come from among the Jews, and thus, Abulafia could well have been seen as fulfilling that prediction.[3] Though, as promised in Revelation, the Antichrist would, in the end, be defeated, his appearance in Rome might have been viewed by these Joachimites as part of the tribulations due a corrupt church. Abulafia's predictions about the end of Christianity may also have been seen in this light. Thus, aiding Abulafia achieve his announced purpose would be helping to bring about the advent of the new age. Others might have been impressed with his vision of the messianic age, which seemed, to a certain extent, to endorse their own understanding of a coming together of Christians and Jews. They might have been interested to see what would happen when the pope and Abulafia met. The latter might also be true for those who perhaps saw Abulafia as a curious, mad, but entertaining sideshow. While not taking him too seriously, they saw him as an interesting diversion, perhaps much like Sampson, a Jew from Northampton, who in 1277 "assumed the habit of a friar minor, preaching certain things in contempt of the Christian faith and said order."[4] Lastly, Abulafia may also have been seen as a pawn in a much larger political game. Some Franciscans may have seen this as an opportunity to put pressure on the pope to convert the Jews and advance the agenda of their own order at the expense of the Dominicans. It might have been their hope that Abulafia's papal audience would be the final nail in the Jewish coffin.

Abulafia was clearly focused on his perceived purpose which was to have an audience with the pope on a specific day, and everything leading up to the event seems to have been arranged, from his perspective, with some foresight. He arrived in Rome in the month of Ab (July 1280) in order to meet with the pope on the Friday before the Jewish New Year (August 26, 1280). His arrival at least a month before the intended date shows good sense, and may indicate that he believed that he stood a good chance of achieving his objective. This may also attest that Abulafia was aware that there were channels and procedures that needed to be followed in order to receive a papal audience, and that he would have to maneuver carefully in order to get the required date. The fact that he was apprehended by "strangers" in Trani but "miraculously" escaped, and was not stopped anywhere else on the way to Rome and in the city itself is, perhaps, an indication that he had powerful (Christian) protectors who were interested in seeing his mission accomplished.[5] Surely the Jewish communities in Capua and Rome would have done all in their power to stop Abulafia, and the fact that they could not is suggestive. The text in *Sefer ha-Edut* states that the pope had prior knowledge of Abulafia and his purpose but did not want to meet with him. If Abulafia's account is considered trustworthy, this prior knowledge implies that Abulafia had some sort of connections with the papal curia.

Abulafia may have been led to believe by his Franciscan contacts that Nicholas III would grant him an audience. During the 1270s the divide between the conventuals and spirituals was not as great as it would become in the 1280s and 1290s. Given that the lines were not clearly drawn and there were Franciscans of different levels of observance living and working together, some of whom were also Joachimites, Franciscan entreaties to Nicholas to meet with Abulafia might have been expected to receive a favorable outcome. Given the pope's long-time acquaintance, love, and care for the order, the Franciscans involved may have felt that with proper representation, Nicholas would find it difficult to refuse them.

Prior to his becoming Pope Nicholas III, Giovanni Gaetano Orsini had always been closely associated with the order. His father was an acquaintance of Francis, and from 1263 till his accession to the papal throne in 1277, Giovanni was cardinal protector of the order. As pope, he was very involved with the promulgation of the bull *Exiit qui seminat,* which attempted to deal once and for all with, among other things, the question of poverty and the use and ownership of property by the brothers. Nicholas III intended this to be the definitive interpretation of the rule.[6] In 1279 he appointed his nephew, Matthew Rossi, as cardinal protector, and on the occasion supposedly described the order in glowing terms, and the same source also mentions that the order was grieved at Nicholas's death.[7] While Salimbene mentions Nicholas's nepotism, he also states that the latter was friendly with John of Parma, a friendship that presumably began when he was cardinal protector of the order, though he clearly was not happy with his Joachimism, which he referred to as sayings of fools. Salimbene records a conversation between John of Parma and Nicholas III that must have taken place between 1277–1280 in Rome, where the former castigated the latter for being more concerned with wars and other trifles than saving souls.[8] Perhaps the context for this conversation was the intense activity in the summer of 1279 leading to the publication of *Exiit qui seminat.* Interestingly, though supposedly under house arrest at the hermitage in Greccio, John of Parma was clearly a pretty regular visitor to the Roman Curia as he was also there in 1276–1277 with Pope John XXI who wanted to appoint him cardinal.[9] Other members of the family, such as Giovanni's nephew Lord Jacopo Colonna, were also on excellent terms with John of Parma and the former was appointed cardinal by his uncle in 1278.[10]

Additional evidence also suggests that Nicholas III's negative reputation is dependant on events that occurred after the latter's death with the increased tensions between spirituals and conventuals, and might not truly reflect Nicholas III's real interests and views.[11] It is of interest that both of the series of prophecies that eventually became known as the *Vaticinia de summis pontificibus* are not overtly critical of Nicholas III, at least not in comparison to the following popes. The "Ascende Calve" series probably authored in Provence between 1328–1330 by a Franciscan spiritual with a good knowledge of papal history, do not paint a negative picture of Nicholas though it is clear that he is the source of the forthcoming evil.[12] Even one of the leading spirituals in the early fourteenth century, Ubertino de Casale, while critical of *Exiit qui seminat,* did not portray Nicholas III as an enemy of the faithful, though this might have been because of the continued protection given him by the pope's nephew.[13] Hence, while not sympathetic to the teachings of Joachim of Fiore, it would seem that Nicholas III was not opposed to the spirituals, and when pope he still met with central figures such as John of Parma notwithstanding the latter's Joachimism.

Jerome d'Ascoli (the future Nicholas IV), unlike Nicholas III, was a prominent member of the Franciscan Order. He had progressed within the ranks of the order from lector to provincial minister, and in 1274, he replaced Bonaventure as minister general, and continued in that position until the general chapter, which took place in Assisi in May 1279, where he was allowed to resign. As provincial minister during the early 1270s, he would have surely had a copy of the *Legenda maior* written by Bonaventure and ratified by the chapter in 1266 as the official life of the founder of the order.[14] The introduction of that work teaches that the end of times is near and that Francis was the sixth angel of the apocalypse, and had a central place in the history of salvation. Even if this apocalyptic reading of Francis's life was interpreted in various ways and the element of apparent crises absent for many, this would still have been the basis of Jerome's understanding of Francis and the role of the order.[15] Jerome was appointed cardinal in 1278 by Nicholas III, who, as previously noted, had himself been the cardinal protector of the Franciscans until his election to the papacy.[16] Jerome was an efficient minister general of the order, though mostly *in absentia,* because he was constantly dispatched on diplomatic missions to the

Eastern Church, and to France. After Bonograzia of St. John in Persicuto was elected minister general, Jerome went to Rome where he worked on the commission that produced *Exiit qui seminat* in August 1279.[17]

Jerome's position on the issue of extreme poverty and observance is difficult to judge. From his attitude toward Peter John Olivi both when minister general and pope, and depending on which sources are used, he was either condemnatory or laudatory.[18] He supposedly worked together with Peter John Olivi during the summer of 1279 in Rome, though he had condemned one of Olivi's treatises on the Virgin Mary to the flames, but he also later recommended him as lector to the friars in Florence.[19] As pope, Jerome had a complicated relationship with Raymond Geoffroi, minister general of the order from 1289, who owned a copy of Joachim's *Concordia,* was supportive of the spirituals, and sent Olivi back to Montpellier. Thus, there might be reason to suppose that Jerome would have been marginally interested in meeting a Jew espousing eschatological teachings with Joachimite leanings, who had been recommended to him by brothers in the order.

More importantly, as has already been mentioned, Peter John Olivi was in Rome in the summer months of 1279 and was part of the consultation team dealing with the bull *Exiit qui seminat.*[20] Olivi wrote important treatises on Franciscan poverty, which are part of a larger work, *Questiones de perfectione evangelica,* which attempts to present Olivi's vision of the totality of Christian life.[21] Olivi's views on the Virgin Mary had been censured by Jerome, but he must have regained enough favor to be invited by the provincial minister of Provence, Bermond d' Anduze, to submit his work as part of the consultations in preparation for the publication of the bull.[22] Olivi was influenced by the writings of Joachim of Fiore and also envisioned the conversion of the Jews as happening within history and before the Last Judgment and of being crucially important for the correction of the carnal Church. He also talks about the conjoining of Jews and Gentiles and their becoming one flock.[23] It is difficult to imagine that while in Rome, Olivi limited himself to discussing the issue of poverty alone, and it is reasonable to assume that his teachings on apocalyptical themes made the rounds of Franciscan circles in that city.[24] This may also go a long way to explaining why some of the Franciscans in Rome were so eager, less than one year later, to see what would happen when Abulafia met with Nicholas III.

The Jewish network revolves around scholars with whom Abulafia studied or taught in the Iberian Peninsula and Italy.[25] In *Otzar Eden Ganuz,* Abulafia mentions that he taught the *Guide* to two of the elders of the Jewish community of Rome, Rabbi Zedekiah and Rabbi Yeshayah (Isaiah) of Trani.[26] Rabbi Zedekiah was scion of one of the leading Roman Jewish families, the Anaw, who traced their ancestry back to one of the families deported by Titus to Rome. The family was prominent in the community during the second half of the thirteenth century. His father and uncle, Benjamin and Abraham, were both doctors. Zedekiah, who died after 1280 (but before late 1285) had relatives such as Shabbethai Anaw who was a close companion of Zerahiah ben Shaltiel Hen, and the latter translated philosophical works for him. Another cousin was Zedekiah, son of the aforementioned Abraham, the author of *Shibolei ha-Leket,* an impressive attempt to codify the Halachah. Yeshayah was from Trani and was a leading Halachic authority.[27] Abulafia refers to both Zedekiah and Yeshayah as being very old, and also mentions that both the latter had some success in their studies, implying that Abulafia was already teaching his Kabbalistic interpretation to the *Guide.* He also refers to them as his allies, implying that there were those in Rome who, perhaps not surprisingly, were not that well disposed toward him. This seems to indicate that Abulafia had already announced himself as Messiah, meaning that this stay in Rome was after 1276.[28] Zedekiah, with his family connections, and Yeshayah with his Halachic reputation, would have been well placed to help Abulafia when he arrived in Rome in 1280. His relationship with these two figures is an indication that Abulafia had well-placed acquaintances and prior knowledge of the makeup of the Jewish community before his arrival in 1280.[29]

Prior to this reference to the stay in Rome, Abulafia mentions that: "I was in the town of Capua about five days journey from

Rome, and I found there an honourable wise and clever man, a philosopher and doctor and his name was Hillel and I joined him and learned philosophy from him. . . ."[30] This was just after Abulafia's trip to the Holy Land in 1260. Hillel can easily be identified as Hillel ben Samuel of Verona who was one of the central figures involved in the controversy over Maimonides' works. Hillel was very supportive of Maimonides and was active as a teacher and commentator of his works in the late thirteenth century. He was also clearly connected with Christian scholars as he translates works from Latin into Hebrew, among them, the first chapter of Thomas Aquinas's *Tractatus de unitate intellectus contra Averroistas,* composed in 1270.[31] The latter is to be found in his philosophical compendium *Tagmulei ha-Nefesh,* completed in Forlì in 1291, which deals with the issues of the immortality of the soul and reward and punishment.[32] Hillel was part of a group of scholars including Zerahiah ben Shaltiel Hen and Maestro Gaio who propagated the works of Maimonides in Italy, though there were severe differences of opinion among the group. Hillel studied in Barcelona in the early 1260s with Rabbi Jonah Gerondi (d. 1263), but spent most of his life in Rome, Capua, Forlì, and Ferrera.[33] Abulafia's enthusiasm for the *Guide* was definitely inspired by Hillel, though the disciple went much farther than his teacher in interpreting the secrets of the *Guide.* While Abulafia studied with Hillel in the 1260s, there is good reason to believe that the two remained in contact and perhaps were together in Capua in 1279 when Abulafia composed the second of his three commentaries on the *Guide.*[34] A letter written by Zerahiah to Hillel indicates that he disapproved of Abulafia's approach to the *Guide,* but implies that Hillel was aware of his commentaries, which were written in the 1270s and 1280s.[35] Hillel regarded himself as the best reader of the secrets of the *Guide,* though he clearly faced stiff competition from Abulafia.[36] The secrets tackled by Hillel are reminiscent of what Abulafia tries to do; the purpose is the same (to reach the ultimate truth); the content is, however, different.[37]

The aforementioned Zerahiah was one of the leading exponents of Maimonides in Rome in the late thirteenth century. He was born in Barcelona, scion to an important family, and moved to Rome in 1277 where he was active as a philosopher, commentator, teacher, and translator, mainly from Arabic.[38] He also wrote an important commentary to the *Guide for the Perplexed*.[39] Zerahiah's extant correspondence shows that he was in touch with Maestro Gaio as well as with his cousin, Judah Salmon, who lived in Barcelona. The latter is important because he also studied the *Guide* with Abulafia and because he is the addressee of a letter from Abulafia written in the late 1280s, defending his messianic claims and teachings against the attack spearheaded by Solomon ibn Adret. Zerahiah was also in contact with Hillel of Verona, though with the latter the relations turned from friendship to acrimony particularly over the issue of the interpretation of Maimonides' *Guide*.[40] Zerahiah did not think very highly of Hillel's abilities as a philosopher, nor, not surprisingly, was he enamored by Abulafia's reading of Maimonides' *Guide*. His reaction to Abulafia's arrival in Rome in the summer of 1280 might have been so negative as to include warning his Christian contacts against him. From Abulafia's point of view, this would not have necessarily been such a bad thing. Negative publicity is still publicity, and it would have meant that highly placed Christians would have knowledge about his mission.

Not much is known about Isaac b. Mordechai, or Maestro Gaio, aside from the fact that he was doctor to popes and cardinals, among them Jerome d'Ascoli.[41] It seems that aside from Maimonides, he was also interested in Islamic medical treatises as there is a record of Nathan de Cento (ha-Meati) translating Ammar ibn Ali al-Masuli's work on eye diseases "for his friend Isaac."[42] There are a couple of extant letters from Hillel of Verona (ca. 1220–ca. 1295) to Maestro Gaio dealing with the renewed controversy over Maimonides' works in the late 1280s. Interestingly, in one of his letters, Hillel regrets the fact that Maestro Gaio, then in Rome, had not sent him the letter that he had written, and he comments: "And why and for what reason [the letter was not sent] I will not enquire or try [to guess], because maybe I know [the reason] and it is permissible to be reticent, and to comment is forbidden." And farther on in the letter, he talks about himself as an expert on the

Guide, and he comments that: "I was taught these issues from a special Rabbi."[43] While inconclusive, given that Abulafia had studied with Hillel before 1270, and after he left Spain he returned to Italy and wrote commentaries on the *Guide,* it is possible that the former disciple had become teacher. It might be possible, therefore, that both the comments in this letter are veiled references to Abulafia. Interestingly, in the early 1290s, Maestro Gaio is known to have gained Nicholas IV's support for the Jews of Rome who were being mistreated by the clergy, who were violating their rights and depriving them of their property.[44] Hence, it is possible that he may have also used his connections with Jerome d'Ascoli to pique his interest regarding Abulafia and his request to meet with Nicholas III.

It is possible that here is to be found Abulafia's entrée to the papal court. Through Maestro Gaio's connections with Jerome d'Ascoli and perhaps other cardinals such as Jacobo Colonna, along with Abulafia's own interaction with the Franciscans, there was a perceived opportunity for a papal audience. According to Abulafia's version of events, when he arrived at Rome the pope was already at Soriano.[45] Abulafia made no secret of his intentions, as seen in the *Sefer ha-Edut* where, according to his account, the pope commanded his gatemen not to allow Abulafia entry into the papal residence. This refusal and the advice of his associates did not deter Abulafia who, believing he was on a Divine mission, was determined to carry it out. Yet again, Abulafia showed foresight by coming to Soriano a few days prior to when he hoped for an audience, perhaps depending on a papal change of heart. "On the day of his going before the Pope," the morning of Friday, August 23, as Abulafia approached the papal residence, he was informed that Nicholas III had succumbed suddenly and died during the night, from causes unknown.[46] As has already been suggested, the pope's death was interpreted by Abulafia as Divine retribution for refusing to meet Abulafia and as a clear sign that the power of Christianity was waning. It is possible that the messenger who came out to meet him could have been one of his Jewish or Franciscan acquaintances who would have been aware of Abulafia's impending arrival.

Presumably, Abulafia returned to Rome, as did the papal curia for the burial of the pope, which took place on August 25, and spent the days leading up to, and the new year (August 27–28) with the Jewish community. It was only on August 29 that he was "detained" at the Franciscan house, probably the Arcali (Ara Coeli) on the Capitol, given to the Franciscans in 1249.[47] Remaining in Rome for the New Year's celebrations was not the behavior of one who thought that he was in any imminent danger. Abulafia's reaction to his "apprehension" by the friar minors and his stay with them is also devoid of any negativity. One would expect that had the episode been traumatic, and given Abulafia's opinion about Christianity, he would have been more vitriolic about the Franciscans and the whole affair.

Hence, there are two plausible explanations for what happened. The first is that Abulafia was detained by elements in the order opposed to Joachimite teachings, who, given that the former openly preached about his impending meeting with the pope and the approaching end of Christianity, may have wanted to make sure that he had not had a hand in the pope's sudden death. Having interrogated Abulafia and discovered that he was essentially harmless, and perhaps not entirely sane, they then freed him. This reading receives some support in that Abulafia remarks that he was detained for twenty-eight days, the number being numerically equal to the name Jesus and the important term *potentia* (*koah*).[48] Thus, Abulafia might be implying that he had been able to defeat the forces of Christianity, and that indeed, their power had come to an end.

The second and more intriguing possibility is that he was cautiously welcomed by the Franciscans who were interested in his papal mission, and who may have shared his belief that the end of days was fast approaching. Given Abulafia's lack of discretion prior to his proposed papal audience, they wanted to make sure that no harm befell him in the aftermath of Nicholas III's death. This reading also receives support from the passage in that Abulafia does not write that he was imprisoned, but rather that "he stayed in their *collegium* (*ve-amad be-midrasham*)." The Franciscan prisons were not known for their creature comforts and surely would have merited a mention if that is where he had spent this period. This seems to imply that he was not actually in prison, but staying in the *collegium* itself with the friars.

The records that have survived about the late-thirteenth-century Franciscan houses in Rome are patchy and make it difficult to determine who the brothers were and whether they were inclined to Joachimite speculation. However, it is reasonable to assume that given the proliferation of Franciscan Joachimites all over Italy and beyond, there must have been some in Rome. Salimbene reports that the copy of Gerard of Borgo San Donino's *Eternal Gospel* that he had burned belonged to a Roman senator, which, along with all the other evidence mentioned above, seems to indicate that there was an interest in Joachimism in Rome. Thus, either of the aforementioned scenarios is possible. However, in the end, Nicholas III's refusal to meet with Abulafia was of little consequence.[49] The news about the death of the pope, which Abulafia received as he approached the papal residence, was a clear signal for Abulafia that God's will had been done. Abulafia did not wait around to meet with the next pope; he would have had to wait half a year anyhow and from his perspective there was no need to do so. God and his "Antichrist" had announced to all and sundry that the power of Christianity was at an end and that the true Messiah was soon to be revealed. Thus, what might have been perceived by some to be a complete failure in that he did not actually meet with the pope, was presented by Abulafia as a total triumph.

Conclusion

In one of his later works, Abulafia recalled a public disputation that he had with a certain wise Christian, probably in southern Italy or Sicily. There were many other Jews and Christians in attendance, and according to the account, all present had agreed that only the participants were to speak without any interruptions from the audience. The first part of this description is reminiscent of the depiction of the setting in the Christian account of the Barcelona disputation, while the latter element brings to mind the request of the Gentile and the agreement of the three wise men in Ramon Llull's *Llibre del gentil e dels tres savis.*[1] However, the way the specific question Abulafia deals with is posed suggests that this Christian was neither a Friar Paul nor a Ramon Llull. The issue at hand does not focus on a particular text, but deals with the question of why the stories about the forefathers are included in the biblical text. This is an issue that was generally not raised in Christian-Jewish debates, and is very different from the approach Llull would have adopted.[2]

The Christian asked: "Did the forefathers and all the other figures who lived before Moses and the giving of the Law achieve the perfection that the Torah, once it was given, intended, from then till now, and from now till eternity, or did none of them achieve that perfection?"[3] Abulafia understood the question to imply that if it was possible to achieve perfection before the Torah was given, what need was there for the Torah in the first place, and if they did not achieve perfection, then the only possible purpose for telling these stories was to point at some future perfection. The way that the question was posed by the Christian brings to mind Joachim's exegesis of the biblical text. Though Abulafia does not give the

Christian much room to expound his views, one could imagine him going on to explain the importance of the forefathers and their *concordia* with central figures of the New Testament, the second status, pointing to the spiritual perfection in the third status. Thus, Abraham and Zachary, Isaac and John the Baptist, Jacob and Christ gaze into each others faces and indicate the progression from flesh to spirit.[4] Abulafia's response negates the Joachimite reading by implying that the forefathers' perfection was based on oral knowledge of the true inner meaning of the Torah as revealed to them by God. He uses Jacob's dream of the ladder connecting between heaven and earth to get the Christian to admit that it is a prophetic revelation of the perfection that can be achieved by those who seek the true Divine essence, each according to his ability.[5] The giving of the Torah on Sinai was in order to provide a teaching aid for the achievement of perfection not just of individuals but for a whole nation, and thus the Torah is a witness to the special status of the Jews.[6] Hence, the Joachimite explanation offered by the Christian of a future perfection intimated by the stories of the forefathers is negated by exalting their high level of perfection in that they received revelation and knew the truth, which is revealed by the Torah. Unremarkably, in the Abulafian account of this disputation, the Christian congratulated Abulafia on his explanation and accepted it as much more convincing than his own reading. He then continued to study with Abulafia and presumably accepted his understanding of the Torah and the fast-approaching end.

This disputation with the Christian is representative of the processes described in this book. Well grounded in his own religious traditions and teachings, Abulafia was able to appropriate contemporary Christian ideas, fusing them with his own revelations, and coming out with a vibrant and engaging apocalyptic and messianic scenario which he was certain would attract his Jewish contemporaries and hoped would also convince Christians. From the date of the expected redemption to the coming together of Jews and Gentiles and the inclusiveness of the new age, Abulafia's engagement with the apocalyptic teachings of some of his Christian contemporaries enriched his own worldview. Though his messianic claims were a result of his revelatory experiences and hermeneutical reading of the Torah, they were, to no small extent, dependent on his historical circumstances and acculturation.

In a study of this nature, what constitutes proof of contact or influence between the different elements involved? Naturally, it would be nice if we could point to a text that clearly spells out the nature of the contacts between Abulafia and the Franciscans, or perhaps, if we could find a source in which Abulafia cites directly from Joachim's works. Given the relative paucity of textual evidence of that sort, it would perhaps be easier to say that there was no point of meeting at all and that the coincidences in dating, end of world predictions, and the expected scenario are no more than that. Yet, as the circumstantial evidence accumulates and the picture becomes clearer, it is difficult to avoid the conclusion that Abulafia saw the inherent possibilities in Joachim's teachings, as they were understood and adapted by his Franciscan contemporaries, in furthering his own mission and messianic claims.[7]

Abulafia's willingness to openly discuss and reveal the secrets of the Divine name was based on the belief that the end was nigh. Joachim's teachings about the end were based on the same premise *quia tempus prefinitum adest* (for the predefined time has arrived).[8] Abulafia's prediction of the date of his coming as the Messiah, though based on his own interpretation of the biblical text, was the same as the one adopted by Joachimite supporters after 1260 with reference to the Anno Domini. The Joachimite determination is based also on a hermeneutical reading of the biblical texts by the medium of spiritual intelligence. Abulafia embraces Joachim's understanding of the relationship between the Jews and the Christians only to turn it on its head, though he also posits reconciliation at the end of days. Abulafia's adoption of the persona of the prophet Zechariah at a crucial moment in his messianic career would also seem to be a polemical stance against the claims for Joachim as an alter-Jeremiah.

Abulafia spent much of his most creative period in Sicily and southern Italy, the area in which Joachim himself lived and taught and one of the main centers of diffusion of his works. The geographical proximity along with Abulafia's predilection for preaching to Jews and Christians alike, coupled with the Franciscans' stated mission to the Jews makes it hard to believe that there would have been no contact between them. At one juncture, Abulafia actually mentions the Franciscans by name as well as relating that he spent almost a month in their company. There may be different ways of interpreting this meeting of minds, yet when both text and context are taken into account, the burden of proof would seem to be on those who deny this meeting ever took place. Apocalyptic beliefs are very powerful motivators, and at this juncture, where two competing belief systems met, the battle lines were drawn, and the results, at least on the Jewish side, were spectacular.

It is perhaps not surprising that the apocalyptic and messianic tension evident in Abulafia's writing and activities is not what was emphasized by most of his disciples and adherents, both historically and today. That tension only truly makes sense within its particular historical context, as it is a response to the cultural milieu in which it was formulated. With the passing of time, these elements of his thought became incomprehensible, and, therefore, were negated or ignored. When considering apocalyptic material trying to uncover the historical context in which it was formulated and decipher the symbols used is crucial for understanding the motivations and beliefs of the usually anonymous authors. In Abulafia's case as well, the historical context is so important because, without it, central aspects of Abulafia's life and messianic claims make little sense. For instance, why was the year 5050 AM (1290 AD) so important? What was so special about that particular year? The historical context in which Abulafia thrived and developed provides the framework for understanding these issues. However, in following generations, the focus would change to Abulafia's goal of achieving individual perfection, the techniques for receiving prophecy and attaining *unio mystica,* rather than on the apocalyptic elements.

In a footnote to her book *The Figurae of Joachim of Fiore,* dealing with the connection between Joachim and the Jewish convert Peter Alphonsi, Marjorie Reeves cites Gerschom Scholem's negation of any connection between late-thirteenth-century Kabbalists in Spain and the disciples of Joachim. She writes: "Scholem concludes that there is little probability of a direct historical connection between the seer 'in far-off Calabria' and the Spanish Cabbalists. But the fact of Joachim's relationship with Petrus Alphonsi puts the whole question in a new perspective. There seems little doubt that Joachim drew on Jewish mysticism through the converted Spaniard. Is it not possible that at a later date, there was again cross-fertilization, perhaps in this case an influence of Joachites upon Jewish thought rather than the other way around?"[9] While one could perhaps argue with the premise regarding the influence of Jewish mysticism on Joachim, this book shows that the hunch of that doyen of Joachim studies in modern times was spot on, but perhaps not exactly in the way she envisioned.

Notes

Introduction

1. On the writing of counterhistory, see A. Funkenstein, *Perceptions of Jewish History* (Berkeley: 1993), 36–40, 70–87, 169–201. Funkenstein points out (80–81) just how few genuine Jewish apocalypses there were and jumps from the First Crusade to Shabbatai Zvi, the latter of course being a messianic apocalyptic eruption. With a different emphasis on counterhistory as bringing to light a subterranean history, a secret tradition, see D. Biale, *Gerschom Scholem: Kabbalah and Counter-History* (Cambridge, MA: 1982), 6–8.
2. M. Landauer, *Literaturblatt des Orients* 6 (1845), 380–83, 417–22, 471–75, 488–92, 507–10, 525–28, 556–58, 570–74, 588–92, 747–50; H. Graetz, "Abraham Abulafia, der Psuedomessias," *Monatsschrift für Geschichte und Wissenschaft des Judentums* 36 (1887): 557–58. See also the strange, but quaint description of Abulafia and his Kabbalistic system in C. D. Ginsburg, *The Kabbalah: Its Doctrines, Development, and Literature* (London: 1920), 194–98 and B. Pick, *The Cabala: Its Influence on Judaism and Christianity* (Chicago: 1913?), 40–42.
3. *Ve-Zot le-Yehudah* (And This Is for Judah), in A. Jellinek, *Auswahl Kabbalistischer Mystik* (Leipzig: 1853); *Sheva Netivot ha-Torah* (Seven Paths of the Torah), in *Philosophie und Kabbala,* ed. A. Jellinek, Leipzig: 1854; "*Sefer ha-Ot.* Apokalypse des Pseudo-Propheten und Pseudo-Messias Abraham Abulafia vollendet im Jahre 1285," in *Jubelschrift zum Siebzigsten Geburstage de Prof. Dr. H. Graetz* (Breslau: 1887), 65–88 (Hebrew section). See also R. Keiner, "From *Ba'al ha-Zohar* to Prophet to Ecstatic: The Vicissitudes of Abulafia in Contemporary Scholarship," in *Gershom Scholem's Major Trends in Jewish Mysticism 50 Years After,* ed. P. Schäfer and J. Dan (Tübingen: 1993), 146–52.
4. G. Scholem, *Major Trends in Jewish Mysticism* (Jerusalem: 1941), 119–55 and his lecture series *The Kabbalah of Sefer ha-Temunah and Abraham Abulafia,* ed. I. Ben Shelomo (Jerusalem: 1987). Even in his thematic

articles dealing with broad swathes of Kabbalistic material where Scholem adopts a phenomenological approach, Abulafia and ecstatic Kabbalah are not mentioned. See M. Idel, *The Mystical Experience in Abraham Abulafia* (Jerusalem: 1988), 10. See also M. Idel, "The Contribution of Abraham Abulafia's Kabbalah to the Understanding of Jewish Mysticism," in Schäfer and Dan, 117–43.

5. Any research on Abulafia has to start with Moshe Idel's PhD thesis, *R. Abraham Abulafia's Works and Doctrines* (Hebrew) (Hebrew University 1976). For the three volumes of essays based on the thesis and many other relevant articles and books, see the notes and bibliography of this book.
6. E. Wolfson, *Abraham Abulafia—Kabbalist and Prophet: Hermeneutics, Theosophy, and Theurgy* (Los Angeles: 2000).
7. G. Scholem, *The Messianic Idea in Judaism and other Essays on Jewish Spirituality* (New York: 1971), 1–36, particularly 15–16 (again, no mention whatsoever of Abulafia); Biale, *Gershom Scholem,* 71–78.
8. M. Idel, *Hasidism: Between Ecstasy and Magic* (New York: 1995), 22–23 suggests that the historical method is problematic ("in many cases 'history' stands for the shaky picture accepted by one scholar on the basis of the writings of another . . . collected sometimes according to a preconceived theory about the social, political, or economic situation") and not very useful when applied to mystical texts.
9. See M. Idel, *Messianic Mystics* (New Haven and London: 1998), 63, 65–79.
10. See B. McGinn, *Visions of the End: Apocalyptic Traditions in the Middle Ages* (New York: 1998), xvi–xx, 1–36; the introduction to the third edition of N. Cohn, *The Pursuit of the Millenium: Revolutionary Millenarians and Mystical Anarchists of the Middle Ages* (London: 1970), 13–16 and E. Weber, *Apocalypses: Prophecies, Cults, and Millenial Beliefs through the Ages* (Toronto: 1999).
11. S. M. Wasserstrom, *Between Muslim and Jew: The Problem of Symbiosis under Early Islam* (Princeton: 1995), 77–82.
12. See also M. Goldish, *The Sabbatean Prophets* (Cambridge, MA: 2004) who succeeds in doing for Sabbatianism what I have tried to do here with Abraham Abulafia.
13. See also S. Sharot, *Messianism, Mysticism, and Magic: A Sociological Analysis of Jewish Religious Movements* (Chapel Hill: 1982) 45–61.
14. Short sections of parts of Abulafia's works have been translated mainly into English. See for instance A. Kaplan, *Meditation and Kabbalah*

(Northvale, N.J.: 1995), 84–106; B. Bokser, *The Jewish Mystical Tradition* (Northvale, N.J.: 1993), 98–106; L. Jacobs, *The Schocken Book of Jewish Mystical Testimonies* (New York: 1997), 72–80; R. Patai, *The Messiah Texts* (Detroit: 1988), 178–80; J. Dan, *The Heart and the Fountain: An Anthology of Jewish Mystical Experiences* (Oxford: 2002), 121–27. In the early part of 2007, a number of translations of Abulafia's works have appeared published by Providence University. These translations are linked to a website www.everburninglight.org. Among the translated works are *Sefer Ha-Ot, Get ha-shemot* and *Sheva Netivot ha-Torah*. *Ner Elohim,* a work by one of Abulafia's disciples is published as a work by Abulafia himself.

15. See *Hayei ha-Olam ha-Ba,* 9–22.
16. The serious differences are relatively few and have more to do with the medieval copyists of Abulafia's works than with the modern editors. Abulafia enjoys playing with Latin and Greek words, writing them out in Hebrew orthography in order to tease out their true meaning. A copyist without the necessary background scrambled these words. However, they can normally be pretty easily be reconstructed by working backward from the "true" Hebrew meaning Abulafia gives these terms.
17. There are some sixty manuscripts containing this work.

Chapter 1. Joachim and Joachimism in Italy

1. For a general overview of Joachim's biography, see B. McGinn, *The Calabrian Abbot: Joachim of Fiore in the History of Western Thought* (New York and London: 1985), 1–47; R. Lerner, *The Feast of St. Abraham: Medieval Millenarians and the Jews* (Philadelphia: 2001), 5–22; and G. Luca Potesta, *Il Tempo dell'Apocalypse: Vita di Gioacchino da Fiore* (Rome and Bari: 2004), among others.
2. Since the research carried out by M. Reeves and B. Hirsch-Reich, *The Figurae of Joachim of Fiore* (Oxford: 1972) it is the general consensus of opinion that the *Liber figurarum* was written by Joachim or one of his close disciples with later additions by scribes.
3. Joachim's concordance between the twelve tribes and twelve churches is more sophisticated in that he divides them each into two groups of five and seven. There were five tribes who received their inheritance first and they represent the primary, outer, literal, and

active. The other seven tribes who received their inheritance later represent the secondary, inner, spiritual, and contemplative. Corresponding to this are the five churches designated by Peter that hold primacy, while the seven churches of Asia designated by John receive their spiritual inheritance later. Naturally, there are also five bodily senses and seven spiritual gifts as well. This exemplifies the Joachite conception of progression from the material to the spiritual of both the individual and history. See M. Reeves, "The *Liber Figurarum* of Joachim of Fiore," *Medieval and Renaissance Studies* 2 (1950): 78–79.

4. Ten of the twelve tribes were lost in the time of King Uziah as a result of the Assyrian conquest, and according to Joachim, ten of the twelve churches disappeared during the persecutions of the Arians and Barbarians. See McGinn, *The Calabrian Abbot,* 182–92; Lerner, *The Feast of St. Abraham,* 12–14. See *Liber figurarum,* Corpus Christi College, Oxford Ms. 255A, ff. 10v–11r.
5. See St. Augustine, *City of God against the Pagans,* ed. and trans. R. W. Dyson (Cambridge: 1998), book 20.
6. *Liber concordia,* translated in B. McGinn, *Apocalyptic Spirituality: Treatises and Letters of Laetantius, Adso of Montier-en-Der, Joachim of Fiore, The Spiritual Franciscans, Savonarola* (Mahwah, New Jersey: 1979), 124.
7. Mat. 17:1–8; Luke 9:28–35; Mark 9:2–8.
8. Mat. 17:12–13. See also Luke 1:17 based on Malachi 3:23–24 and Mat. 11:14. M. Reeves, *The Figurae,* 196–97 and *Influence,* 16–20.
9. *Liber de Concordia Novi ac Veteris Testamenti.* Ed. E. R. Daniel. *Transactions of the American Philosophical Society,* 73. Philadelphia: 1983 (the first four books), 79, cited also in B. McGinn, *The Calabrian Abbot,* 125: "[T]he spiritual understanding proceeding from both Testaments is one that pertains especially to the Holy Spirit."
10. Joachim took this idea and his spelling of the Tetragrammaton from Peter Alfonsi's *Dialogue against the Jews.* See Reeves, *Figurae,* 44; J. Tolan, *Petrus Alfonsi and His Medieval Readers* (Gainesville: 1993), 114. G. Luca Potesta stresses the importance of the Hebrew alphabet in general for Joachim as the letters appear (in Latin inscription) in a number of figures. He also suggests that the wise Jew mentioned by Joachim may have been influential in developing Joachim's presentation of the Tetragrammaton, and that Joachim may have met him while Alexander III's papal court was in Verona (between 1184–1187). Joachim was in Verona in 1186 just as he was putting together these ideas for the first time. See Luca Potesta, *Il Tempo dell'Apocalypse,* 130–35. See also B. Hirsch-

Reich, B. "Joachim von Fiore und das Judentum." In *Judentum im Mittelalter,* ed. P. Wilpert and P. Eckert. Berlin: 1966, 230–36.

Pope Innocent III also adopts this spelling of the Tetragrammaton and explication of the Trinity from Joachim. See F. Robb, "Did Innocent III Personally Condemn Joachim of Fiore?" *Florensia* 7 (1993): 82–87.

There has been speculation as to whether Joachim had Jewish origins. See H. Grundmann, *Ausgewählte Aufsästze,* vol. 2, *Joachim von Fiore* (Stuttgart: 1977), 323–41; Hirsch-Reich, "Joachim von Fiore und das Judentum," and recently in Lerner, *The Feast of St. Abraham,* 24–29.

11. Joachim of Fiore, *Expositio in Apocalypsim,* (Venice: 1527) ff. 34v–36v and the *Psalterium Decem Chordarum.* Ed. and trans. E. Russo. Chiaravalle Centrale: 1983, 326–29. See Reeves, *Figurae,* 38–51.
12. *Psalterium decem chordarum,* 485.
13. Oxford, Corpus Christi College Ms. 255A, f. 8r. The Reggio Emilia manuscript, which is very similar in design to the Oxford manuscript, has an empty space where the IEUE should be. Reeves explains this change in connection with the Trinitarian polemic with Peter Lombard. See Reeves, *Figurae,* 200–202.
14. Oxford, Corpus Christi College Ms. 255A, f. 7v. The circles with the Tetragrammaton also appear in manuscripts of other works such as in the *Expositio in Apocalypsim.* See the diagrams at the end of Reeves, *Figurae,* figures 3, 26, 27.
15. The importance of the Tetragrammaton is emphasized in the sentences written above and below the four large letters IEVE in the figure. Above the central letters is Exodus 6:3, "And I appeared to Abraham, to Isaac and to Jacob as God Almighty, but by my name IEVE, I did not make myself known to them." In other words, this name was the special name revealed to the redeemer, Moses. Underneath the letters, Joachim writes: "Hoc est ineffabile nomen Dei, quod gerebat in fronte Aaron summus pontifex, scriptum quatuor litteris in hac pagina insignitis, propter quod et a Grecis tetragrammaton nominatur." Referring to Exodus 28 or 39 dealing with the *tzitz* which the high priest wore on his forehead when in the temple, which had special significance. See A. Patchovsky, *Dei Bildwelt der Diagramme Joachims von Fiore: Zur Medialität religiös—politischer Programme im Mittelalter* (Berlin: 2003), 93.
16. According to the figure of the beast in the *Liber figurarum,* the seventh head is the minor Antichrist, the tail represents Gog, the ultimate

Antichrist, and the space between the seventh head and the tail represents the third status. Thus, for Joachim, there will be two Antichrists. See Reeves, *Figurae,* 151–52.

17. Oxford, Corpus Christi College Ms. 255A, f. 7r. See also Reeves, *Figurae,* 136–38.
18. *Liber concordia,* f. 56r. See Reeves, *Influence,* pp. 395–97; McGinn, *The Calabrian Abbot,* 112–13; and Reeves, *Joachim of Fiore and the Prophetic Future,* 14. This is not, however, the angelic pope, a concept that does not directly appear in Joachim's authentic works. Reeves, *Influence,* 399 explains that first the revolutionary idea of a transition to the third status had to be developed, then when the idea that the papacy would be seized by demonic forces caught on, the idea of an angelic pope could develop in the late thirteenth century.
19. Reeves, *Influence,* 28–36. See also F. Robb, "The Fourth Lateran Council's Definition of Trinitarian Orthodoxy," *Journal of Ecclesiastical History* 48 (1997): 22–43.
20. Reeves, *Influence,* 146.
21. An example of this is the Oxford compilation of the *Liber figurarum* dated to the early thirteenth century, which is from the south of Italy as is the Reggio Emilia manuscript (ca. 1250–1270). Both these manuscripts are very similar and had a common source. The Oxford manuscript also contained the *Liber concordia* (or parts of), one of Joachim's works on the apocalypse, and the *Psalterium.* See M. Reeves, "The *Liber Figurarum* of Joachim of Fiore," *Medieval and Renaissance Studies* 2: 58–59.
22. See M. Reeves, "The Abbot Joachim's Disciples and the Cistercian Order," *Sophia* 19 (1951): 355–71 and her *Influence,* 149–58; S. E. Wessley, *Joachim of Fiore and Monastic Reform* (New York: 1990), 101–35; R. Moynihan, "The Development of the 'Pseudo-Joachim' Commentary 'Super Hieremiam': New Manuscript Evidence," *Mélanges de l'Ecole Française de Rome, Moyen âge—Temps modernes* 98 (1986): 109–42.
23. Joachim of Fiore (Pseudo), *Super Hieremiam Prophetam.* Venice: 1516, ff. 11v, 14r, 45v–46v. Frederick II is described as *"leo saevus de aquilone," "regulus colubri."* See Reeves, *Influence,* 307; R. E. Lerner, 'Frederick II, Alive, Aloft, and Allayed, in Franciscan-Joachite Eschatology," in *The Use and Abuse of Eschatology in the Middle Ages,* ed. W. Verbeke et al. (Leuven: 1988), 359–81. Frederick II's role—his conflict with the

papacy was so well known that a Muslim writer could record a conversation between Frederick and a dignitary called Fakhr al-Din b. al Shaykh about the caliph and the pope and have Frederick saying: "What a good thing that [the Caliphate] is. But those people of limited intelligence—meaning the Franks—take an ignorant and dull-witted man from the dunghill—there is no relationship between him and the Messiah—[and] they make him a caliph over them, taking the position of Messiah over them, whilst your caliph is the scion of the uncle of the Prophet, and he is the person most worthy of his position." Ibn Wasil, *Mufarrij ak-kurub,* ed. J. al-Shayyal, IV (Cairo: 1953–1957), 251, translated in C. Hillenbrand, *The Crusades: Islamic Perspectives* (Edinburgh: 1999), 320. Ibn Wasil died in 1298.

24. For more on the recalculation to 1290, see the text below around n.36. See Reeves and Hirsch-Reich, "The *Figurae* of Joachim of Fiore Genuine and Spurious Collections," *Medieval and Renaissance Studies* 3 (1954): 177–82 particularly the descriptions of Ms. Vatican Lat. 3822 and Ms. Paris, Bibl. Nat., Lat. 3595. On the composition of the Isaiah commentary between 1260–1266, see Lerner, "Frederick II, Aloft," 378, no. 61.

25. For the encyclical, see R. J. Armstrong, ed., *Francis of Assisi,* Vol. 2, *The Founder* (New York: 2000), 771–72; Reeves, *Influence,* 146. For the Franciscan interest in Joachite teachings see also B. McGinn, "Apocalyptic Traditions and Spiritual Identity in Thirteenth-Century Religious Life," in *Apocalypticism in the Western Tradition* (Aldershot: 1994), VII, 6–17.

26. See Bonaventura, *Legenda maiora,* trans. B. Fahy, in *St. Francis of Assisi: Writings and Early Biographies,* ed. M. A. Habig (Quincy, IL: 1991), 631–32. On Bonaventura's Joachimism, see Reeves, *Influence,* 179–80; McGinn, *The Calabrian Abbot,* 213–19: and J. Ratzinger, *The Theology of History in St. Bonaventure* (Chicago: 1989).

27. See D. Abulafia, *Frederick II: A Medieval Emperor* (London: 1988), 325, 331.

28. Salimbene de Adam, *The Chronicle of Salimbene de Adam,* trans. J. L. Baird (New York, 1986): 228. On Salimbene and Joachimism, see D. C. West, *Joachimism and Fra Salimbene,* PhD thesis, UCLA (Los Angeles: 1970), his "The Education of Fra Salimbene of Parma: the Joachite Influence," in *Prophecy and Millenarianism: Essays in Honour of Marjorie Reeves,* ed. A. Williams (London: 1980), 191–215 and

"Between Flesh and Spirit: Joachite Pattern and Meaning in the Cronica of Fra Salimbene," *Journal of Medieval History* 3, no. 4 (1977): 339–52.

29. See E. R. Daniel, "A Re-examination of the Origins of Franciscan Joachitism," *Speculum* 43 (1968): 671–76. For Abraham Abulafia's extended visits to Capua, see the following chapter. On the early history of the Franciscans in Sicily particularly in Messina and Palermo, see Filippo Cagliola, *Almae Siciliensis Provinciae Ordinis Minorum Conventualium S. Francisci* (Venice: 1644, fasc. Palermo: 1984), 43–60, 91–94. Cagliola cites from earlier sources such as papal missives and Wadding as well as from local manuscripts.
30. See Salimbene de Adam. *The Chronicle of Salimbene de Adam.* Trans. J. L. Baird. New York: 1986, 83: "And it is now the year 1283, the feast of St Gorgon the martyr, and Martin IV is currently Pope."
31. See D. Burr, *The Spiritual Franciscans: From Protest to Persecution in the Century after Saint Francis* (University Park, PA: 2001), 1–41, M. D. Lambert, *Franciscan Poverty: The Doctrine of Absolute Poverty of Christ and the Apostles in the Franciscan Order 1210–1323* (New York: 1998), 109–31.
32. See McGinn, *The Calabrian Abbot,* 127–28 for places where Joachim's language could lead to misunderstanding regarding a new Gospel.
33. Gerard was allowed to continue teaching until 1257 when the general chapter meeting in Rome tried him, and again in 1258 in Paris by Bonaventure. See Lerner, *The Feast of St. Abraham,* 145, 47. On the Commission of Aragni, see H. Denifle, "Das Evangelium acturnum und die Commission eu Prasni" *Archivsür Literatur und Kirchengeschicchte des Mittelalters,* 1 (1885): 49–142.
34. Reeves, *Influence,* 62–63. He writes a number of treatises against the mendicants and more particularly against their adoption of Joachite teachings, and identifies them with the forces of the Antichrist. Following 1260 he or someone familiar with his early works denigrates Joachim as a false prophet as the events prophesied did not occur. However, he too believes that the end of days is fast approaching. See A. G. Traver, "The *Liber de Antichristo* and the Failure of Joachite Expectations," *Florensia* 15 (2001): 87–98.
35. Salimbene, *Chronicle,* 466. Needless to say that Salimbene warned against reading the book and had the copy burned.
36. The prediction appears in the pseudo-Joachimite commentary on Isaiah. *Super Esaiam prophetam,* ch. 16, f. 30v. See B. Töpfer, *Il regno futuro della libertà* (Genoa: 1992), 157 who corrects the date given in

the printed edition and Lerner, "Frederick II," 378 no. 60 who cites from an early manuscript corroborating the correction. See also Lerner, *The Feast of St. Abraham,* 55 and n.40 below.

It is possible that John of Parma also accepted the recalculation of the generations and looked forward to 1290. Ubertino of Casale mentions that in 1285 he was with John of Parma at Greccio and the latter told him: "Within four years, God will tell you explicitly whom you should follow and whose word of truth should be followed without hesitation." When Ubertino heard of John's death four years later he interpreted those words as meaning that he should follow John of Parma who had predicted his own death. However, John may have been referring to events he expected to take place in 1290 in light of this recalculation of generations. See Ubertino de Casale, *The Tree of the Crucified Life of Jesus,* in *Francis of Assisi: Early Documents—The Prophet,* ed. R. J. Armstrong et al. (New York: 2001), 151–52.

37. Salimbene, *Chronicle,* 228–29.
38. Ibid., 302. See Salimbene, *Chronicle,* 235 where Hugh of Digne states that Frederick II is still alive.
39. Indeed, Salimbene was in Ferrara when Innocent IV preached and talked about Frederick's death, and when Brother Gerardino of Parma punched him on the arm and told him to give up his study of Joachim now that the emperor was dead, Salimbene did not say anything. It would have been the perfect place to announce his renunciation of Joachim. Salimbene, *Chronicle,* 455. See also p. 164 where Salimbene registers his horror at the early and unexpected death of Frederick II: "When I heard this, I was horrified and could scarcely believe it. For I was a Joachite and I fully believed and even hoped that Frederick would do even greater wicked deeds in the future . . ."
40. Salimbene, *Chronicle,* 474–77 and 566 respectively.
41. Ibid., 646.
42. See *Super Esaiam prophetam,* ch. 20, f. 31v, and also in the pseudo-Joachim, *Epistola subsequentium figurarum,* Ms. Vatican Lat. 3822, f. 3r-v where the New Testament generations are calculated from the Passion rather than the nativity. See Reeves, "The *Figurae* of Joachim of Fiore," 179–82. Both these collections seem to have been written in southern Italy presumably after 1260 and show an active school of Joachimist thought in the areas that Abulafia would have frequented. Reeves points to the Cistercians as being responsible for

these collections, which, naturally, does not imply that they would have been unknown outside the monastery. See Reeves, *Figurae,* 288–89. Lerner, "Frederick II," 378 n.60 suggests that Salimbene had clearly lost interest in Joachim after 1260 as he does not cite the Isaiah commentary. If my reading is correct, then this seems to indicate that Salimbene was aware of the recalculations and had not lost interest in Joachim.

43. When Salimbene was writing, there indeed was no emperor. There, were, however, Kings of the Romans which is the title given to the German king who has not been crowned by the pope. The next emperor would be Henry of Luxembourg (Henry VII) who would be crowned by instruction of Clement V in Rome in 1312. See M. Barber, *The Two Cities: Medieval Europe 1050–1320* (London and New York: 1992), 222–23.
44. Salimbene, *Chronicle,* 503–506.
45. *Liber concordia,* 130, 158–59, also cited in Lerner, *The Feast of St. Abraham,* 24.
46. *Liber figurarum,* Ms. Oxford, Corpus Christi College, 255A, f. 12v. This figure known as the Trinitarian tree has the names of the sons of Noah in Hebrew lettering, however, after close examination of the Hebrew letters, I am of the opinion that they are a much later addition to the figure. See Reeves, *Figurae,* 170–73 and for a picture of the figure, plates 18, 19 and p. 27 of this book. On the union of Gentiles and Jews, see Lerner, *Feast of St. Abraham,* 23–37; E. Randolph Daniel, "Abbot Joachim of Fiore and the Conversion of the Jews," in *Friars and Jews in the Middle Ages and Renaissance,* ed. S. J. McMichael and S. E. Myers (Leiden: 2004), 1–21; and A. Sapir Abulafia, "The Conquest of Jerusalem: Joachim of Fiore and the Jews," in *The Experience of Crusading,* Vol. 1, *Western Approaches,* ed. M. Bull and N. Housley (Cambridge: 2003), 127–46. See also J. Cohen, "*Synagoga Conversa:* Honorius Augustodunensis, the Song of Songs, and Christianity's 'Eschatological Jew,'" *Speculum* 79 (2004): 332–34 where he questions Joachim's originality on the issue of the Jews at the end of time. See also A. Blank, "Trinität und Geschichte in Joachim von Fiores *Psalterium decem chordarum,*" *Florensia* 10 (1996): 161–63.
47. See *Super Esaiam prophetam*, ff. 48v, 49v and Lerner, *Feast of St. Abraham,* 55–56.
48. See Joachim of Fiore, *Tractatus super Quatuor Evangelia,* ed. E. Buonaiutu (Rome: 1930), 101–102, 109, 140, 143, 151, 229, 310–24. See

also the Italian translation, Gioacchino da Fiore, *Trattati sui quattro Vangeli,* trans. L. Pellegrini (Rome: 1999), 78, 101, 107, 215–16, 223.

49. Salimbene, *Chronicle,* 505–506. This comment follows a citation of Luke 2:46 and could well refer back to the *Treatise.* See Gioacchino da Fiore, *Trattati sui quattro Vangeli,* 28–29. See also Reeves, *Figurae,* 97, n.100. See *Chronicle,* 294 where Salimbene states that he received the commentary from Hugh of Digne in 1248 and made a copy for John of Parma.
50. Salimbene was on friendly terms with a Jew named Yom Tov (Diesbene) who sat next to him in church to hear a sermon. See *Chronicle,* 396.
51. This document was published by C. Baraut, "Las antiguas biografias de Joaquín de Fiore y sus fuentes," *Analecta Sacra Tarraconensia* 26 (1953): 207–25 and then by H. Grundmann, "Zur Biographie Joachims von Fiore und Rainers von Ponza," *Deutsches Archiv für Erforschung des Mittelalters* 16 (1960): 437–564. A new and superior edition with an Italian translation was published by S. Oliverio, "*Vita beati Joachimi Abbatis,*" *Florensia* 16–17 (2002–2003): 220–40. This *Vita* is only known from a sixteenth-century manuscript made by Cornelius Pelesius, the prior of the monastery in Fiore in the late 1500s.
52. S. Wessley, "The Role of the Holy Land for the Early Followers of Joachim of Fiore," in *The Holy Land, Holy Lands, and Christian History* (*Studies in Church History* 36), ed. R. N. Swanson (2000), 185.
53. Interestingly, Salimbene cites Frederick II who "either jokingly or seriously, believing it to be the truth, . . . used to say in insult to God, that He had not seen his kingdoms of Sicily, Calabria or Apulia, else He would never have commended the promised land so highly." Frederick knew what he was talking about as he had been to the Holy Land in the 1220s. Salimbene, *Chronicle,* 559.
54. See Wessley, "The Role of the Holy Land," 181–191 and his "The True and New Jews: Jerusalem Rebuilt," *Frate Francesco: Rivisti de cultura francescana* n.s. 70, no. 2 (2004): 285–314.
55. *Liber concordia,* 402.
56. Reeves, *Influence,* 13–14. The commentary to Jeremiah posits that a pope will be killed and that there will be no pope at the time of the Antichrist, when Pilate rules with the support of the Jews. See *Super Hieremiam,* f. 53r (translated in Mcginn, *Visions of the End,* 189–90). See also B. McGinn, "Angel Pope and Papal Antichrist," in *Apocalypticism in the Western Tradition* (Aldershot: 1994), V, 156–59.

57. Reeves, "The *Figurae* of Joachim of Fiore," 183, 194–98. *Premissiones,* preceding the *Super Esaiam prophetam,* beneath the figure of the seven seals. For an examination of Joachim's treatise on the seven seals, see J. E. Wannenmacher, *Hermeneutik der Heilsgeschichte. De septem sigillis und die sieben Siegel im Werk Joachims von Fiore* (Leiden: 2005).
58. See the preface of the *Super Hieremiam* among others. Reeves, *Influence,* 397–98.
59. Salimbene mentions the book three times in the *Chronicle* and indeed he is the first to refer to it by that name. See Reeves, *Figurae,* 112, n. 76.

Chapter 2. A Life Reviewed

1. See among others J. N. Hillgarth, *The Spanish Kingdoms 1210–1516,* Vol. 1 (Oxford: 1976), 234–62; D. Abulafia, *The Western Mediterranean Kingdoms 1200–1500* (London and New York: 1997), 28–56.
2. See Y. Baer, *A History of the Jews in Christian Spain* (Philadelphia: 1992) and Y. T. Assis, *The Golden Age of Aragonese Jewry: Community and Society in the Crown of Aragon, 1213–1327* (London: 1997).
3. On the so-called "Maimonidean controversy," see J. Sarachek, *Faith and Reason: The Conflict over the Rationalism of Maimonides* (Williamsport: 1935); Y. Baer, *A History of the Jews in Christian Spain,* Vol. 1, 96–110; A. Neuman, *The Jews in Spain,* Vol. 2 (Philadelphia: 1969), 117–45; D. J. Silver, *Maimonidean Criticism and the Maimonidean Controversy 1180–1240* (Leiden: 1965).
4. See G. Scholem, *Origins of the Kabbalah* (Princeton: 1990); M. Idel, *Kabbalah: New Perspectives* (New Haven and London: 1988); and H. Hames, *The Art of Conversion: Christianity and Kabbalah in the Thirteenth Century* (Leiden: 2000), 31–82 and the bibliography cited there.
5. On Nahmanides, see C. Henoch, *Nahmanides: Philosopher and Mystic* (Jerusalem: 1978); E. Wolfson, "By Way of Truth: Aspects of Nahmanides' Kabbalistic Hermeneutic," *AJS Review* 14 (1989): 103–78; M. Idel, "Nahmanides: Kabbalah, Halakhah, and Spiritual Leadership," in M. Idel and M. Ostrow, *Jewish Mystical Leaders and Leadership in the 13th Century* (Northvale, NJ: 1998), 15–96; H. Pedaya, *Nahmanides: Cyclical Time and Holy Text* (Hebrew) (Tel Aviv: 2003), 86–119; and M. Halbertal, *By Way of Truth: Nahmanides and the Creation of Tradition* (Hebrew) (Jerusalem: 2006), 297–352. For a fascinating examination of the social and cultural symbiosis between Jews

and Christians in Barcelona, see E. Klein, *Jews, Christian Society, and Royal Power in Medieval Barcelona* (Ann Arbor: 2006).

6. Others followed in his footsteps, for instance David ha-Reuveni. See A. Z. Aescoli, *Jewish Messianic Movements: Sources and Documents on Messianism in Jewish History from the Bar-Kohba Revolt until Recent Times* (Hebrew) (Jerusalem: 1987), 368–69 and p. 145 n. 1 in this book.
7. One exception being the third and last of the three short works that make up the book now known as *Sefer ha-Ot* written in 1288.
8. Abulafia's year of birth is always given as AD 1240 which corresponds with 5000 AM. However, the Jewish New Year falls normally circa September in the previous year, so there is an overlap of a few months of the Jewish year with the previous Julian calendar year (in the Mediterranean world, the new year in the Julian calendar, actually started on the March 25, which corresponds, more or less, to the month of Nissan in the Jewish year). In *Sefer ha-Ot,* pp. 81, 85, Abulafia writes: "A new vision was revealed to me on the fourth of the seventh month which is the first month of the start of the eighteenth year of my visions," and that he completed the book "in the year *heh mem het* [=48]." The first part dates the vision to 4 Tishrei of the eighteenth year, which is the start of 5048, in other words around September 14, 1287. This means that his first vision was in Tishrei 5031, which corresponds to September–October 1270. In *Otzar Eden Ganuz,* p. 369, Abulafia writes that "when I was *aleph lamed* (31) years old in the city of Barcelona, God awakened me from my sleep." For Abulafia to have been thirty-one in Tishrei 5031 AM and born in 5000 AM, he must have been born in late AD 1239. Additionally, in *Sefer ha-Edut,* p. 57, Abulafia writes that wrote *Sefer ha-Yashar* in 5039 when he was thirty-nine years old, and it was the ninth year since the start of his prophecies, which began in Barcelona in 5031, i.e., late 1270, again implying that he was born in late 1239 after the start of Jewish New Year 5000.
9. *Otzar Eden Ganuz,* 368. Almost all the modern editions of Abulafia's works are edited by A. Gross. Therefore, I have not given the full bibliographical details here, unless the work was edited by someone else. Full references are to be found in the bibliography.
10. See I. J. Yuval, "Jewish Messianic Expectations towards 1240 and Christian Reaction," in *Toward the Millenium: Messianic Expectations from the Bible to Waco,* ed. P. Schäfer and M. Cohen (Leiden: 1998),

105–21 and his *"Two Nations in Your Womb": Perceptions of Jews and Christians in Late Antiquity and the Middle Ages* (Berkeley and Los Angeles: 2006): 258–266. See also S. Shalev-Eyni, "Cosmological Signs in Calculating the Time of Redemption: The Christian Crucifixion and the New Moon of Nissan," *Viator* 35 (2004): 265–287.

11. *Otzar Eden Ganuz,* 368. Ishmael referring to the Mamluks, Esau to the Mongols.

12. See Patai, *Messiah Texts,* 181, 183. In Hebrew, the idea is first found in a ninth-century work written by one Eldad ha-Deni. See A. Epstein, "The Story of Eldad ha-Deni" in *The Writings of Abraham Epstein,* Vol. 1, ed. A. M. Haberman (Jerusalem: 1950), 83–138. See also A. Neubauer, "Where Are the Ten Tribes?" *Jewish Quarterly Review* 1 (1888–89): 14–28, 95–114, 185–201, 408–23 and A. Gow, *The Red Jews: Antisemitism in an Apocalyptic Age* (Leiden: 1995), 29–42. Meshullam da Piera wrote a poem expressing the sentiment that the Mongols were the ten lost tribes. See Aescoli, *Jewish Messianic Movements.* 214 Around 1260, there were prophecies about the Mongols making the rounds among Christians as well, see F. Schmeider, 'Nota sectam maometicam atterendam a tartaris et christianis:' The Mongols as non-believing apocalyptic friends around the year 1260,' *Journal of Millenial Studies* 1:1 (1998) 1–11.

13. Crusader Acre in the early 1260s would have been an interesting place to be anyhow. Nahmanides' arrival there in 1267 would have had a major impact on the community, but even before that, there was a diverse and impressive Jewish community. Earlier in the century, probably between 1209–1211, a large group of rabbis arrived in the Holy Land and some of their descendants settled in Acre. In the 1230s, the Jews of Acre had been involved in the controversy surrounding the works of Maimonides, with some, likely immigrants from the West, supporting the ban, while others, likely those of Eastern background, proclaiming the greatness of the "Great Eagle." Just prior to Abulafia's arrival, a group of immigrants arrived from France including the son of Rabbi Yehiel of Paris, one of the main protagonists of the trial against the Talmud in 1240. See J. Prawer, *The History of the Jews in the Latin Kingdom of Jerusalem* (Jerusalem: 2000), 244–72.

14. This is the only mention of his spouse in his works. The text suggests that he went directly to the Holy Land, but then says "and I left there

and returned to Greece, where I married a woman on my way." *Otzar Eden Ganuz,* 368. Does this mean on the way to the East, or on his way to study with Hillel in Capua?

15. See Abulafia's comment in *Sheva Netivot ha-Torah,* 112, and also *Ve-Zot li-Yehudah,* 28–29.
16. *Otzar Eden Ganuz,* 368.
17. Hillel mentions that he was in Barcelona for three years studying with Rabbi Jonah Gerondi. This was probably from 1259–1262, as Jonah left Barcelona that year and Hillel mentions that he was in Barcelona at that time. See Hillel's letter in *Igrot Kena'ot,* 14a.
18. His relationship with the latter was more volatile as they disagreed over the interpretation of Maimonides' *Guide for the Perplexed.* There are a number of extant letters that record their correspondence. See also J. B. Sermoneta, "Thine Ointments Have a Goodly Fragrance: Rabbi Judah Romano and the Open Text Method" (Hebrew), in *Shlomo Pines Jubilee Volume,* Vol. 2, ed. M. Idel, W. Z. Harvey, E. Schweid (Jerusalem: 1990), 77–114.
19. See ch. 5 for more discussion of this issue. See also, Y. Schwartz, 'Magic, Philosophy and Kabbalah: The Mystical and Magical Interpretation of Maimonides in the Later Middle Ages (Hebrew),' *Da'at* (forthcoming 2007).
20. Indeed, it seems that this idea of secrets in the *Guide* did not originate with him, and from a remark he makes in *Sitrei Torah* and in *Hayei ha-Nefesh,* it may have been received wisdom, perhaps from Hillel of Verona, though where this tradition originates is difficult to ascertain. See M. Idel, "Abulafia's Secrets of the Guide: A Linguistic Turn," in *Perspectives on Jewish Thought and Mysticism,* ed. A. L. Ivry, E. R. Wolfson and A. Arkush (Amsterdam: 1998), 311–13. See also A. Altmann, "Maimonides's Attitude Toward Jewish Mysticism," in *Studies in Jewish Thought: An Anthology of German Jewish Scholarship,* ed. A. Jospe (Detroit: 1981), 200–219, esp. 206–209.
21. See S. Benjamin, *The World of Benjamin of Tudela: A Medieval Mediterranean Travelogue* (London: 1995), 57–61. See S. P. Bensch, *Barcelona and its Rulers, 1096–1291* (Cambridge: 1995), particularly 277–346. On the Jews of Barcelona see the excellent, but still unpublished dissertation by L. Berner, *On the Western Shores: The Jews of Barcelona during the Reign of Jaume I, "el Conqueridor," 1213–1276* (PhD dissertation, UCLA) (Los Angeles: 1986).
22. *Ve-Zot le-Yehudah,* 29.

23. See H. J. Hames, "A Seal within a Seal: The Imprint of Sufism in Abraham Abulafia's Teachings," *Medieval Encounters* 11, no. 4 (2006), 153–72. See also F. M. Tocci, "Dottrine 'Eremetich' tra gli ebrei in Italia fino al Cinqucento," in *Italia Judaica: Atti del 1 Convegno internazionali Bari 18–22 Maggio 1981* (Rome: 1983), 292–96.
24. See G. Scholem, *The Kabbalah of Sefer ha-Temunah and Abraham Abulafia,* 106–107; M. Idel, *Studies in Ecstatic Kabbalah,* (Albany: 1988) ca. p. 76, and his "La història de la Càbala a Barcelona," *Curs la Càbala* (Barcelona: 1985), 59–74. See also S. Blickstein, *Between Philosophy and Mysticism: A Study of the Philosophical-Qabbalistic Writings of Joseph Giqatila (1248-c. 1322,)* (PhD dissertation, Jewish Theological Seminary) (1983), 92–123, who suggests that Togarmi along with Moshe de Leon, Abraham Abulafia, and Joseph Gikatilla constituted a Kabbalistic school or circle and wrote what Blickstein refers to as philosophical-Kabbalistical works. Togarmi's only extant work, *Maftehot ha-Kabbalah* (a commentary to *Sefer Yetzira*), can be consulted in Scholem, *The Kabbalah of Sefer ha-Temunah and Abraham Abulafia,* 229–39.
25. See *Ve-Zot le-Yehudah,* 16 and *Otzar Eden Ganuz,* 32–33 for a similar list of commentaries.
26. See the very important study of H. Pedaya, *Vision and Speech: Models of Revelatory Experience in Jewish Mysticism* (Los Angeles: 2002), 191–97.
27. *Sheva Netivot ha-Torah,* 125. See also *Ve-Zot le-Yehudah,* 18–19. Moshe Idel has suggested that Abulafia was also influenced by Ashkenazi material that he encountered in Rome in 1279–80. See M. Idel, "From Italy to Ashkenaz and Back: On the Circulation of Jewish Mystical Traditions," *Kabbalah* 14 (2006): 91–2.
28. Though it is important to emphasize that his understanding of the Sefirot is very different from that of his theosophical colleagues. See Wolfson, *Abraham Abulafia,* 94–177.
29. See Pedaya, *Vision and Speech,* 194 for an analysis of why this vision is most likely to have happened in Barcelona.
30. The thirty-two paths of wisdom mentioned in *Sefer Yetzirah.* There are three main parts signified by the three-word title: The first part (*Otzar*—Treasure) is a commentary on *Sefer Yetzirah,* the second (*Eden*—the Garden of Eden) astronomical calculations dealing with the new moon, and the last part (*Ganuz*—Hidden) dealing with the Divine names. These are accompanied by a short introduction and a last chapter that are central as they encapsulate and demonstrate what Abulafia has shown in the rest of the work.

31. In *Sefer ha-Ot,* Abulafia also portrays himself as a shepherd. The use of the shepherd imagery is interesting in the context of building a portrait of leader and messiah—Moses, David, Jesus.
32. In *Otzar Eden Ganuz,* 9, Abulafia reveals that the name *El* also contains within it thirty (the numerical value of the *lamed*) sefirot, ten in each dimension of soul (humankind), universe (creation), and year (time) taken from *Sefer Yetzira,* and the thirty are one signified by the *aleph*. So it is an important name in itself.
33. See *Otzar Eden Ganuz,* 382 where Abulafia describes the seventh level of reading the Torah as being called "Holy of Holies." It is this level of reading that Abulafia achieved at this time. The same depiction of the seventh level as being the "Holy of Holies, only for prophets and the circle that encompasses all others" is also found in *Sheva Netivot ha-Torah,* 92.
34. *Otzar Eden Ganuz,* 374. See, for example a passage from *Sefer Hayei ha-Nefesh* dealing with the binding of Isaac, translated in M. Idel, *Language, Torah, and Hermeneutics in Abraham Abulafia,* (Albany 1989) 61—"This then brings about dependence on the two inclinations which undoubtedly are the intellect and the imagination, both of which are angels [Divine messengers]. Although one is a good angel and the other is its opposite, the one an angel, the other Satan, both together exist for the good of the species . . . one is called the angel of death, and Satan, and evil inclination; and the other is called Angel of God. . . ." See also in *Otzar Eden Ganuz,* 41: "The 'dimyon—imagination' [spelled *dalet-mem-yud-vav-nun*] imagines, and its secret is daemon [spelled *dalet-yud-mem-vav-nun*] and the devil and Satan." *Hayei ha-Olam ha-Ba,* 53 where Satan is identified with the woman, as something that seduces the human intellect. See also *Mafteah ha-Tochehot,* 66–67.
35. *Sheva Netivot ha-Torah,* 113.
36. See *Mafteah ha-Tochehot,* 68–69 where Abulafia describes the battle between the intellect and imagination when receiving prophecy, and compares them to the two cherubs on the ark in the Holy of Holies. It is only when the prophet hears the voice coming from between the two cherubs that he has reached the highest level of prophecy. Presumably this is what happens to him in late 1285. See also M. Idel, *Absorbing Perfections: Kabbalah and Interpretations* (New Haven and London: 2002), 406, 438–48.
37. For Abulafia's relations with his students, see farther on in this chapter around n. 88.

38. *Otzar Eden Ganuz,* 370.
39. Abulafia's comment is based, in my opinion, on Nahmanides' interpretation to Leviticus 26:16 which analyzes the differences between the anathemas of Leviticus 26 and those of Deuteronomy 28. Nahmanides claims that the first set of anathemas refers to the first temple, the exile, and subsequent redemption and the second set to the present exile and the future redemption. Hence, Abulafia's intimation that he was working to bring the second curse / anathema to a close.
40. On the German pietists, see I. Marcus, *Piety and Society: The Jewish Pietists of Medieval Germany* (Leiden: 1981); J. Dan, *Hasidism in Medieval Germany* (Hebrew) (Tel Aviv: 1992). See also D. Abrams, *Sexual Symbolism and the Account of the Chariot in Medieval Germany: A Study of the Sod ha-Egoz Texts* (Tübingen: 1997) and D. Abrams and I. Ta-Shma (intros.), *Sefer Gematriot of R. Judah the Pious* (Los Angeles: 1998).
41. Abulafia writes about his students: "And in Barcelona there were two: one was a great and old man, R. Kalonymos, may his memory be blessed. The other was an intelligent, understanding and honourable man from a good family, and his name was R. Judah, whose cognomen was Salmon, and his studying was crowned with great success. And in Burgos there was a teacher and student, the former named R. Moshe Çinpael, a great and distinguished wise man. And the latter was called R. Shem Tov, also a good and nice man, however his youth was a stumbling block and he and his teacher only received some superficial Kabbalistic teachings. And in Medinaceli [in Castile] there were also two: one was R. Samuel the prophet and he was taught a few Kabbalistic matters. The other is R. Joseph Gikatilla, may the one above guard him, and his achievements in what he studied with me were without doubt wonderful, and he added a great deal to them from his own potential and knowledge, and God was with him." See *Otzar Eden Ganuz,* 369. See also M. Idel, "Maimonides" *Guide for the Perplexed* and the Kabbalah," *Jewish History* 18, no. 2–3 (2004): 206–209. Idel suggests that Abulafia taught for seven years, and wrote his three commentaries in this period. Idel also points out Abulafia's importance for the history of the early teaching and reception of the *Guide.*
42. For more on this matter, see the last chapter of this book.
43. See C. Wirszubski, *Pico della Mirandola's Encounter with Jewish Mysticism* (Cambridge, MA: 1989), 89–90, and Abraham Abulafia, *Sefer ha-*

Geulah, ed. R. Cohen (Jerusalem: 2001), 19–20. *Sefer ha-Geulah* is different from the other two later commentaries in content and style. Abulafia mentions that people refer to him as a heretic and epicurean (p. 5), which perhaps reflects his reputation prior to his messianic claims, and fits nicely with his image as teacher of Maimonides in a unique way. Abulafia also makes reference to *Mafteah ha-Ra'ayon* (p. 33) as a book where he deals with the names of all the letters of the Hebrew alphabet. The text seems to give the impression that the latter book was recently composed. See also C. Wirszubski, "Liber Redemptionis—the Early Version of R. Abraham Abulafia's Kabbalistic *Commentary on the Guide for the Perplexed* in the Latin Translation of Flavius Mithridates," *Divri ha-Akedemia ha-Leumit le-Ma'daim* 3 (Jerusalem: 1970): 139–49.

44. See *Sefer ha-Melamed,* 36. On p. 13, Abulafia mentions *Get ha-Shemot.*

45. See for instance *Get ha-Shemot,* 30: "And now I will inform you that the whole world is dependent on it, it is the beginning of all beginnings and the purpose of all purposes, and it is the ineffable Name one in all manners of unity. . . . And it is YHWH . . . and know that this blessed name includes all the other divine names and all emerge from it." See also *Mafteah ha-Ra'ayon,* 66, *Sefer ha-Melamed,* 7–13 among others. Joseph Gikatilla who studied with Abulafia around this period also focuses on the Tetragrammaton in his *Ginat Egoz,* and also makes use of Eleazar of Worms *Sefer ha-Shem* (Book of the Name). Gikatilla still viewed the Tetragrammaton as central in his later works, for instance in *Sha'arei Orah,* p. 48 where he writes: "Know that all the Holy Names mentioned in the Torah are all dependant on the four lettered name (Tetragrammaton) YHWH. . . . And the Holy Names are all dependant on the name YHWH and all are united in it."

46. Abulafia mentions at the start of *Get ha-Shemot* that he does not intend to reveal any secrets regarding the true Kabbalah, a clear indication that it was an early work, as after 1276, Abulafia's reticence leaves him entirely. *Get ha-Shemot,* 2. In addition, the Tetragrammaton remains the ineffable name in that it is unpronounceable, whereas much of Abulafia's messianic understanding after 1276 is based on his knowledge of how to pronounce the Tetragrammaton.

47. The vision occurred in a place named Debon or Debone. The book itself was written in Patras but it is tempting to suggest that this vision took place in the Val Demone in Sicily. The Hebrew has Debone

which could be a scribal mistake as *bet* and *mem* are relatively easy to misread. The Val Demone was the Arabic name of the northeastern part of Sicily, the area between Messina and Catania. Abulafia talks about the "town of Debone," perhaps referring to Messina. On the Jewish presence there since the eleventh century, see M. Gil, "The Jews in Sicily under Muslim Rule in the Light of the Geniza Documents," in *Italia judaica: Atti del I convegno internazionale, Bari 18–22 Maggio 1981* (Rome: 1983), 89. However, in a conversation Moshe Idel pointed out that Debon is 72 in gematria, perhaps referring to the seventy-two (groups of three) letter name of God. However, nowhere does Abulafia say this explicitely as he does with other names such as "Har Patras (Patras mountain)," which when the letters are rearranged reads "Sefer Torah (Torah scroll)." See *Sefer ha-Yashar,* 98.

48. *Sefer ha-Yashar,* 99–102. See Idel, *Messianic Mystics,*. 298–302 where he interprets the end of this passage as referring to a form of knowledge known by the redeemer. He does not discuss the earlier part of the passage.

49. Abulafia uses the Greek or Latin term ego to refer to himself. In *Otzar Eden Ganuz,* 41, Abulafia explains that the secret of ego is the first word of the Decalogue *anochi*—I, and that its inner secret, which is made up of its letters spelled out in Hebrew, is aleph being one, representing the first sefirah which is separate from all the others, being the spirit of God; *gimel* representing the three elements fire, air and water; and *vav* representing the six sealed endings mentioned in *Sefer Yetzirah.* In addition, the three letters add up to ten (*aleph:*1 + *gimel:* 3 +*vav:* 6 = 10), thus having within themselves the ten sefirot. Thus, referring to himself by the term *ego* incorporates many levels of self understanding and perception.

50. The commentary on *Sefer ha-Yashar* is directly followed by *Sefer ha-Haftarah,* which is the book Abulafia wrote and took with him to Rome especially for the Pope. It also deals with the teaching of the Divine name, something Abulafia refers to as a "new Torah."

51. It is interesting that 1276 was a year with great portent for Christians with a Joachite bent as well. The year began with the untimely death of Gregory X, considered a reformist, because of "the evils of the living," there were floods that did enormous damage, and three other popes were elected in quick succession that year. See *The Chronicle of Salimbene de Adam,* 502–507.

52. More about all these themes in chs 3 and 4 of this book.

53. See J. Starr, "The Mass Conversions of Jews in Southern Italy (1290–1293)," *Speculum* 21 (1946): 203–5. One of the most virulent apostates, Manuforte, was a resident of Trani. See also U. Cassuto, "The Extinction of the South-Italian Academies in the Thirteenth Century" (Hebrew), in *Studies in Memory of Asher Gulak and Samuel Klein* (Jerusalem: 1942), 139–52, J. Shatzmiller, "Les Angevins et les Juifs de leurs états: Anjou, Naples et Provence," in *L' Etat Angevin: pouvior, culture, et société entre XIIIe et XIVe siècle* (Rome: 1998), 291–94.
54. One of Abulafia's disciples in Rome was Yeshaya of Trani, and it is possible that he, being from the town, also had a hand in the so called "miracle." See *Otzar Eden Ganuz,* 368. Matthew Paris relates that the Jews accused of the ritual murder of Hugh of Lincoln in 1255 bribed the Franciscans to intercede and pray for them, and this brought about their release from prison. See H. R. Luard, ed., *Matthaei Parisiensis Monachi Sancti Albani Chronica Maiora* (Rolls Series 57, 7 vols.) (London: 1872–83), Vol. 5, 546.
55. See the previous chapter regarding the Franciscans.
56. *Sitrei Torah,* 17–19.
57. Idel, "Maimonides' *Guide for the Perplexed* and the Kabbalah," 205. Idel suggests that *Hayei ha-Olam ha-Ba* was written while Abulafia was in Rome. His argument seems to be based on the fact that manuscripts of Kabbalistic material copied in the early 1280s in Rome include a short citation from the work. However, Abulafia only gives the year of the composition, not the place. It seems to me that Abulafia would not have had the time to write this work in Rome and it was written either just before or after he left Rome. The latter seems more likely as Abulafia mentions the works he wrote to take with him to Rome, and surely he would have mentioned this work if it had already been composed. See M. Idel, "Abraham Abulafia and Menahem ben Benjamin in Rome: The Beginnings of Kabbalah in Italy," in *The Jews of Italy: Memory and Identity,* ed. B. D. Cooperman and B. Garvin (Bethesda: 2000), 237–51.
58. See *Hayei ha-Olam ha-Ba,* 45: "You will resurrect a multitude of people / it will be in the name of YH / leaping like a lion / in every town and place." Taken from the opening poem to this work, it implies that Abulafia, the Lion, symbol of messianic kingship, is spreading his teaching, which will save a multitude in every place and town.
59. *Mafteah ha-Hochmot,* 49. Abulafia writes that he considered these Christians "*Hasidei umot ha-olam*—the righteous of the Gentiles of

the world." However, what Abulafia means is that they had achieved the second of the three possible types (*Tzadik, Hasid, Navi*—Righteous, Pious, Prophet) of people on the path to perfection; in other words, they had gone beyond the simple meaning of the text.

60. *Sefer ha-Ot,* 76a.
61. On the structure of *Sefer ha-Ot,* see H. Hames, "Three in One or One that is Three: On the Dating of Abraham Abulafia's *Sefer ha-Ot,*" *Revue des Etudes Juives* 165, no. 1–2 (2006): 179–89.
62. Only in one other place does Abulafia refer to himself as Zecharyahu and that is in his last work, *Imre Shefer,* 3. Zecharyahu is one of Abulafia's names for the Messiah and it makes sense that in 1291, at the very end of the last generation of the exile, the Messiah would call himself by his messianic name.
63. See the first chapter of this book.
64. See *Sefer ha-Ot,* 76a: "And the poor to whom he [Zecharyahu] had been sent, and for whom he had been revealed did not take the way he came to heart. And they started to say things about him and his God which should not be said."
65. See H. Hames, "From Calabria Cometh the Law, and the Word of the Lord from Sicily: The Holy Land in the Thought of Joachim of Fiore and Abraham Abulafia," *Mediterranean Historical Review* 20, no. 2 (2005): 187–99.
66. It is difficult to imagine how he existed there, unless he trapped and ate rabbits. The island was totally uninhabited, though in later centuries was used by pirates and fishermen. It is, however, a short boat trip to the mainland. For a late medieval description of the island, see T. Freller, "A German Clergyman in Medieval Malta: The Famous Itinerary of Ludolph von Suchen and the Maltese Islands," *European Journal of Theology* 5, no. 1 (1996): 15–26, particularly 18 [" . . . Prope hanc (Malta) est alia insula Colmat (Comnino) vocatur, in qua sunt tot cuniculi quod eis vix sufficit terra ad inhabitandum . . ."].
67. On the Sicilian Vespers, see S. Runciman, *The Sicilian Vespers* (Cambridge 1958) and D. Abulafia, "The Kingdom of Sicily under the Hohenstaufen and Angevins," in *The New Cambridge Medieval History,* vol. 5, *c. 1198-c. 1300,* ed. D. Abulafia (Cambridge: 1999), 510–15. See also S. Simonsohn, *The Jews in Sicily,* Vol. 1 (383–1300) (Leiden: 1997), liii-lix. C. R. Backman, "Arnau de Villanova and the Franciscan Spirituals in Sicily," *Franciscan Studies* 50 (1990): 6–7 suggests that the Franciscans brought eschatological evangelism with them to Sicily after 1283

from Catalonia where it had been widespread from the 1270s. This raises the possibility that Abulafia had already come across some of these teachings before leaving Catalonia. See also J. Pou y Martí, *Visionarios, Beguinos, y Fraticelos Catalanes (siglos XIII-XV),* with an introduction by A. Hauf i Valls (Alicante: 1996), 119–46.

68. The letter was written in Sicily, where Abulafia spent most of his time in the 1280's. The letter states that the time is nigh for redemption, which also explains why Abulafia is revealing the teachings at this time—this would all seem to point to a date after 1285, probably closer to 1290.
69. See the Introduction to Abulafia's Torah commentary, *Mafteah ha-Hochmot,* 2 where he refers to Ahitub as one of his disciples in Palermo and as a doctor. His brother David, also a doctor, was another disciple, and their father, Isaac was also a physician. Ahitub also translated Maimonides' *Milot ha-Higgayon* (Logica) into Hebrew. See Simonsohn, *Jews in Sicily,* liii.
70. *Ve-Zot li-Yehudah,* 19. See M. Idel, "The Rashba and Abraham Abulafia: The Story of an Ignored Kabbalistic Polemic," in *Atara l'Haim: Studies in the Talmud and Medieval Rabbinic Literature in Honor of Professor Haim Zalman Dimitrovsky,* ed. D. Boyarin et al. (Jerusalem: 2000), 244–45, n. 65.
71. Solomon ibn Adret, *Responsa,* ed. H. Dimitrovsky, Vol. 1 (Jerusalem: 1990), 101–102. See Idel, "The Rashba and Abraham Abulafia," 235–51.
72. *Sefer ha-Heshek,* 97–8 discussed in Idel, "The Rashba and Abraham Abulafia," 238–40.
73. *Mafteah ha-Shemot,* 121.
74. See above, n.30.
75. On the possible influence of ibn 'Arabi on this issue, see Hames, "A Seal within a Seal: The Imprint of Sufism in Abraham Abulafia's Teachings." See note 23 above.
76. Further proof that this is so can be found in the introduction to his commentary on Genesis written in 1289 where he writes: "[A]nd the third is the best of them all, and it is the seventh of all the aforementioned paths, and for all that go in this path it is worthy to renew the world, language and understanding . . . and I have talked about these (paths) in *Otzar Eden Ganuz* and in the commentary to Sefer Yetzirah. . . ." *Mafteah ha-Hochmot,* 27.
77. See *Otzar Eden Ganuz,* 5–6.

78. O. Limor, *Die Disputationen zu Ceuta (1179) und zu Mallorca (1286): zwei antijudische Schriften aus dem mittelalterlichen Genua* (Munich: 1994), 287–88. See the introduction for the background to the disputation and the different personalities involved. It is interesting that one of the figures was a "*ba'al shem*" from the East, i.e., someone who combines names. In *Sheva Netivot ha-Torah,* Abulafia blasts these so called "Masters of the Name." See text around n.84 below.
79. See Starr, "Mass Conversions," 206–11.
80. *Sheva Netivot ha-Torah,* 126. On *hitbodedut* and prophecy in Abulafia, see M. Idel, *Studies in Escatic Kabbalah,* 108–11.
81. See one of Abulafia's disciples' comments on the importance of *Sefer Yetzira* as the basis for prophetic experience in *Ner Elohim,* 81.
82. *Sheva Netivot ha-Torah,* 98–109.
83. See the Introduction to the Torah commentaries, *Mafteah ha-Hochmot,* 2–8, where Abulafia explicitely says that is the only true way to read the Torah.
84. *Sheva Netivot ha-Torah,* 128.
85. *Sefer ha-Ot,* 81b-83b. It is tempting to make more of the sign than is perhaps warranted, though the cryptic style of the text lends itself to this. Doubtless it is based on the mark of Cain in Genesis 4:15. Yet unlike Cain and in close relation to the book of *Revelation,* the men with the sign on their forehead are not those chosen to wander the earth, but those who are among the saved. The sign is on the forehead where the *tefillin*—phylacteries (which are also a symbol)—are worn. Looking carefully at the description of the sign, one is tempted, given Abulafia's predilection for matters Christian, to see in it a counterrepresentation of the visual portrayals of the Crucifixion. "And on his forehead an imprinted (*hatum*) sign in blood and ink on either side, and the image of a letter in the shape of a staff is between them, and it is a very wondrous sign . . . and I saw behold there were like seventy tongues emanating from between the sign on his forehead. He referred to the sign on his forehead as the sign of death, and I called it the sign of life for it turned me from being dead to being alive." (This text has been translated with some differences by J. Dan, ed., *The Heart and the Fountain: An Anthology of Jewish Mystical Experience* (New York: 2002), 122–27, particularly 123.) The letter, possibly the *vav* of the Tetragrammaton, between the blood (matter) and ink (spirit) could visually be like the cross with two figures, perhaps *synagoga* and *ecclesia,* on each side. Like the cross that while representing

the death of Jesus also symbolizes life and hope, this letter brings death to some and eternal life to others. The seventy tongues represent the nations and languages, none of whom are excluded from being able to appreciate the letter for what it really is, unlike Christians who in the past clearly misinterpreted the letter as signifying the cross. The blood and ink also symbolize the struggle between matter and spirit, which is another perennial theme in medieval Christian-Jewish polemic. See among others, S. Lipton, *Images of Intolerance: The Representation of Jews and Judaism in the Bible moralisée* (Berkeley, Los Angeles, London: 1999). For Abulafia, the blood also symbolizes the manifest sense of the Torah and the imagination. See Idel, *Absorbing Perfections,* 442–44.

86. On Yehoel, see Idel, *Messianic Mystics,* 85–94. From older Ashkenazi sources, Yehoel is an early manifestation of the archangel Metatron. Yehoel is also numerically equal to Eliyahu = ben (son) = hu hagoel (he is the redeemer) = 52. Thus, this old man is in fact Elijah, who has been appearing for some years to Abulafia, and who refers to him in the text as "son." So Elijah precedes the coming of the King Messiah who may still be Abulafia, though this is not explicitly stated.
87. *Mafteach ha-Tochehot,* 78–79.
88. *Otzar Eden Ganuz,* 368–69. For an analysis of this passage as being of import for our knowledge of the diffusion of the *Guide,* see Idel, "Maimonides' *Guide of the Perplexed* and the Kabbalah," 205–10.
89. See *Shomer Mitzvah,* 8, 50. Even after the destruction of the temple, the Jews still held onto the traditions of who is a priest or a levite. In medieval Spain, the priestly blessing was performed on Sabbaths and Festivals, while elsewhere in Europe, it was performed only on Festivals in the additional service. During the rest of the year, it is just read out by the cantor during the morning service. However, Solomon came from the Holy Land where the custom was to do the priestly blessing (almost) every morning of the year. See I. Elbogen, *Jewish Prayer in its Historical Development* (Hebrew) (Tel Aviv: 1972): 56.
90. *Sefer ha-Heshek,* 2. The modern editor of the work suggests that it was written in 1280, though the only reference to a date in the book is either late 1280 or 1281 (79). However, it is more likely that this book was written in 1285 because of the names of the disciples.
91. See *Or ha-Sechel,* 4–5. Abulafia indicates that he is unable to remain for much time in Messina at this juncture which may again be a reflection of the campaign being waged against him.

92. Clearly, having seven disciples is significant as this is also the number of disciples that he has in Messina in late 1285 when completing *Otzar Eden Ganuz*. Some of the disciples named then are still his disciples in 1288–1289. See *Otzar Eden Ganuz,* 369–70.
93. *Mafteah ha-Shemot,* 121–22 and for the full list of the names of the disciples involved, *Mafteah ha-Hochmot,* 2. See chapter 4 for a fuller discussion of the connection between Pharaoh, Jesus, and matter.
94. *Imre Shefer,* 50.
95. *Sefer ha-Edut,* 67. See also *Mafteah ha-Tochahot,* 108. See also *Sheva Netivot ha-Torah,* 104.
96. The new year started on the Feast of the Annunciation, March 25 in most parts of Christian Europe from the eleventh century onward. This would continue till the sixteenth century when with the adoption of the Gregorian calendar reforms, the start of the new year went back to being January 1 as it was in the Roman Empire. In Catalonia, the dating of the new year from the Nativity rather than the Annunciation started in the mid-fourteenth century. See A. Capelli, *Cronologia, Cronographia, e Calendrio Perpetuo* (Milan: 1988) and R. L. Poole, *Studies in Chronology and History* (Oxford: 1969).
97. In *Hayei ha-Nefesh,* 30 discussing the secret of the the different parts of the calendar year, Abulafia writes: "[T]he judgement is given in Tishrei, but the carrying out [of the judgement] in Nissan." Farther on (35–36), Abulafia cites the verses from Deuteronomy dealing with the ingathering of the people, saying that this will happen either in Tishrei or Nissan.

Chapter 3. The Politics of Universal Salvation

1. See for instance *Sitrei Torah,* 13–14; *Otzar Eden Ganuz,* 53, *Hayei ha-Nefesh,* 152; *Metzaref la-Kessef,* 12–13. This concept is also the basis of Joseph Gikatilla's *Sha'arei Orah,* written before 1291: "You discover that the whole Torah is woven from the name YHWH, and because of that the Torah is called 'the Torah of YHWH is pure' (Psalms 19:8)." Joseph Gikatilla, *Sha'are Orah,* Vol. 1, 48. On this issue see G. Scholem, *On the Kabbalah and Its Symbolism* (New York: 1965), 37–44.
2. See M. Idel, *Language, Torah and Hermeneutics,* 46–55.
3. In this work there is an urgency that does not appear in the earlier commentaries. One can see an awakening of messianic consciousness,

which colors all that Abulafia is trying to do. This work was written in Capua in the aftermath of the Rome episode along with *Hayei ha-Olam ha-Ba*.

4. Abulafia's broad use of the term *Active Intellect,* in some places equating it with the Torah, probably stems from his adoption of Averroes's understanding of *unio mystica* which Abulafia would have come across either in Samuel ibn Tibbon's works or from his teacher, Hillel of Verona, who copied significant parts of Averroes's treatise on the conjunction with the Active Intellect in his *Tagmulei ha-Nefesh*. See M. Idel, *Studies in Ecstatic Kabbalah* (New York: 1988), 4–11, and endnote 27 on p. 23.
5. *Sitrei Torah,* 14–19.
6. *Sefer ha-Edut,* MS. Roma Angelica 38, ff. 18v–19r; p. 78 in the printed edition.
7. The fourth beast is based on Daniel 7 with reference to Daniel 2. Compare with Revelation 13.
8. See *Sefer ha-Edut,* 64 and see the next chapter for more detailed elaboration. The word *Emet* also contains reference to the year 1290 AD.
9. The letters of *emet* when rearranged form the word *atem* (you). In other words, the truth revealed is that you, i.e., the Christians, are also of the Children of Israel. According to Bonaventure (ob. 1274): "In the seventh age, we know that these things will take place—the rebuilding of the Temple, the restoration of the city and the granting of peace. . . ." Translated by B. McGinn, *Visions of the End,* 200, originally from Bonaventure, Collation 16:7–9, *Opera omnia,* 5:408
10. *Otzar Eden Ganuz,* 178–80. There is only one extant manuscript of this important and extensive work now to be found in Oxford (Ms. Oxford Bodleian, Or. 606), dated to the sixteenth century. A comparison of the manuscript with the printed edition shows no significant errors in the sections cited here.
11. *Otzar Eden Ganuz,* 181.
12. Ibid., 182.
13. Ibid., 182–83.
14. Ibid., 183.
15. Ibid., 184. Interestingly, in Nahmanides' version of the Barcelona disputation in 1263, he uses the idea of habituation to explain how James I, the king presiding over events, could accept the Incarnation as true: "For Your Majesty is a Christian, the son of a Christian, and all your life you have heard the priests who have taught you time and

again about these things [the Incarnation] and you accept it out of habituation (*hergilut*)." C. Chavel, ed., *The Writings of Nahmanides* (in Hebrew), 2 vols. (Jerusalem: 1963), Vol. 1, 310–11. Abulafia's comments about habituation may also be an engagement with Ibn Tufayl's conclusions in his Hayy ibn Yaqzan. See L. Goodman (trans), *Ibn Tufayl's Hayy ibn Yaqzan, a Philosophical Tale* (New York: 1972).

16. *Otzar Eden Ganuz,* 186.
17. Ibid., 189–90.
18. Ibid., 191.
19. For the traditional Christian claim, see J. Cohen, *Living Letters of the Law: Ideas of the Jew in Medieval Christianity* (Berkeley: 1999), 19–71.
20. In a different discussion about the emergence of different nations, Abulafia has recourse to the founder of Christianity, whom he describes as "one special man who came from our nation who for certain reasons left it, and took off one form and put on another." Abulafia accuses him of misleading people, particularly those incapable of knowing the difference, those lacking intellect. Abulafia emphasizes two things in particular that Jesus did that attracted people to him; freeing prisoners and replacing circumcision with baptism. See *Sitrei Torah,* 96–97.
21. Compare with what a student of Abulafia's writes: "Thus, the covenant of the language is in relation with circumcision as it is hinted [in the verse] *mi ya'aleh lanu ha-shamayma* (who will go up to the heavens for us—Deut. 30:12), the first letters [of the words] are circumcision [*milah*] and the last letters are the ineffable name [*YHVH*—the Tetragrammaton]." See *Ner Elohim,* 7–8. For the possible source of Abulafia's understanding of the etymology of *Yehudim*, see Idel, "From Italy to Ashkenaz," 89.
22. *Otzar Eden Ganuz,* 193. See also St. Paul's comment in Romans 9:6.
23. See I. Shagrir, "The Parable of the Three Rings: A Revision of its History," *Journal of Medieval History* 23, no.2 (1997): 163–77. Shagrir cites this passage as an example of the parable, though, as can be seen from the continuation, it does not really fit the model of the parable.
24. The emphasis on the power of the twenty-two letters of the Hebrew alphabet is based on the assumption that of all the languages, it is the only one that is divinely inspired; all the others are conventional. Abulafia understands that all the seventy languages have their roots in Hebrew and that if pronounced correctly, will lead back to that original state. However, because all languages originate from the Hebrew, then the true inner meaning of those languages can only be known

when their scripts and pronunciation are returned to their original state in Hebrew. Thus, Abulafia claims and shows the secret meanings hidden within Latin and Greek, which reveal a dimension unknown to those who do not know Hebrew. See *Or ha-Sechel,* 27–33 and *Sheva Netivot ha-Torah,* 124. See Idel, *Language, Torah, and Hermeneutics,* 3–8, 9. Abulafia shows that the numerical value of *tzeruf otiyot* (letter combination) = 1214 = *shiv'im leshonot* (seventy languages). See also G. Scholem, "The Name of God and the Linguistic Theory of the Kabbala," *Diogenes* 79 (1972): 59–80 and *Diogenes* 80 (1972): 164–94 and U. Eco, *The Search for the Perfect Language* (Oxford: 1995), 32–33.

25. The three virtues are (1) the high level of the people, (2) the language, (3) the script. Earlier in this work Abulafia complains that the Jews no longer know Hebrew and have adopted the languages spoken by the nations amongst whom they are dispersed. *Or ha-Sechel,* 32–33.

26. In *Otzar Eden Ganuz,* the third section called *Ganuz* deals with the Divine name.

27. Safrin's edition has "of the people of God" instead of "sons." M. Idel, *Studies in Ecstatic Kabbalah,* 49 translates here "sons of God." Ms. Vatican Ebr. 233, f. 39v, Ms. Vatican Ebr. 597, f. 38v, and Ms. Biblioteca Palatina Parma, De Rossi 2487, f. 21v all read "*banim le-Adonai*" as I have translated in the text.

28. *Or ha-Sechel,* in the edition by M. Safrin (Jerusalem: 1999), 42–45, and in the Gross edition, 34–35. In *Ner Elohim,* 75, one of Abulafia's disciples takes a more particularistic line explaining that the true religion will be revealed when Elijah comes, and it is clearly that of the prophets with whom God spoke. All the other religions are false. See Idel, *Studies in Ecstatic Kabbalah,* 57, no. 22. On the connection between the author of *Ner Elohim* and Nathan ben Sa'adyahu Harar, another disciple of Abulafia's and the author of *Sha'arei Tzedek* (Gates of Justice), see M. Idel, "Rabbi Nathan ben Sa'adiah Harar, Author of *Sha'arei Tzedek* and His Influence in the Land of Israel" (Hebrew), *Shalem* 7 (2002): 47–58 particulary 55 and n.50. In the figure of the dragon with seven heads, Joachim describes the third status after the fall of the first antichrist in the following terms: "Post ruinam autem huius Antichristi erit iustitia in terra et habundantia pacis. Et dominabitur Dominus a mari usque ad mare et a flumine usque ad terminos orbis [based on Psalm 72:8]. Conflabunt autem homines gladios suos in vomeres et lanceas suas in falces, non levabit

gens contra gentem gladium, nec exercebuntur ultra ad prelium (Isa 2:4). Judei quoque et multe gentes infideles convertentur ad Dominum, et delectabitur universus populus in pulchritudine pacis." The similarities stand out! See Reeves, *The Figurae of Joachim of Fiore,* 151. Compare also with Galatians 4:1–7.

29. See *Sheva Netivot ha-Torah,* 3, where Abulafia explains that the rabbis can only achieve the fourth out of the seven spiritual levels on par with Gentile scholars.
30. See *Imrei shefer,* 69–70: "For the whole world was created by letters and in our language and the rest of the letters, languages and nations are all ordered images in order to be in our image (lit. to be similar to us) . . . but they have no real essence, and they are all the art of deception as is all magic."
31. See Idel, *R. Abraham Abulafia's Works and Doctrines,* 412 where he suggests that Abulafia felt that a new universal religion would appear at the end of days, and that Judaism as it stands is the best option, but still not the pure faith of the end of days.
32. See *Mafteah ha-Hochmot,* 60.
33. See Reeves, "The 'Liber Figurarum' of Joachim of Fiore," 75–77.

Chapter 4. 1280—Rome Revisited

1. b. Talmud *Sanhedrin,* 98a.
2. See I. Knohel, *The Messiah before Jesus* (Hebrew) (Tel Aviv: 2000) and his "On the 'Son of God,' Armilus and the Messiah son of Joseph" (Hebrew), *Tarbiz* 58 (1998): 13–37. *Sefer Zerrubbabel,* in D. Stern and M. J. Mirsky, eds., *Rabbinic Fantasies: Imaginative Narratives from Classical Hebrew Literature* (New Haven and London: 1990), 71–73. See also A. Berger, "Captive at the Gate of Rome: The Story of a Messianic Motif," *Proceedings of the American Academy for Jewish Research* 44 (1977): 1–17.
3. *The Writings of Nahmanides,* 306.
4. *Zohar,* vol. 3, f. 212b. See Idel, *Messianic Mystics,* 121–24 and his *Studies in Ecstatic Kabbalah,* 46. The passage talks about the twenty-fifth day of the sixth month (25 Elul), which will be a Friday and is the actual day Abulafia planned to have his audience.
5. Abubrahim is numerically equal to 266 which is Abraham (248) + 18 which is the numerical value of the Hebrew word *Hai*—alive.

6. See the Introduction to *Metzaref ha-Sechel,* 1–2. In the commentary to one of the prophetic books, *Sefer ha-Brit,* 56, Abulafia writes: "And even though the author [of the original prophetic book] is not the commentator from one perspective, though his name is like that of his master, you can consider that they are the same from another perspective. And there is no doubt that if he is I, then I am him." There then follows the name of the author, Bradhoel b. Devashmael the Spaniard from Tudela in Navarre, which of course is Abulafia's name by numerical equivalence (*gematria*).
7. See *Sefer Ish Adam,* 46–47 where Abulafia gives a list of students which when compared to the list in *Otzar Eden Ganuz* implies that these books were written prior to 1285. In addition Abulafia indicates that he was in Messina and the date was 1282/3. In *Sefer ha-Brit,* 56 Abulafia says that both the original prophetic work and commentary were written in close proximity and in the same town—Messina.
8. See *Sefer ha-Edut,* 61–62.
9. In the *Super Hieremiam* this verse is attributed to the deeds of Frederick II. See Salimbene, *Chronicle,* 191. Abulafia is also clearly engaging with Nahmanides' comment in *Sefer ha-Geulah* (The Book of Redemption) about the end of the exile being near and his subsequent calculation of the approaching end to 1358 based on his understanding of the relevant verses in Daniel, including the one cited here. Nahmanides justifies his calculations in that, unlike the calculations of a great number of rabbis before him, he is actually living at the end of times and the secrets can now be revealed. Abulafia clearly agrees with Nahmanides that the end of times is near, however, he disagrees with his interpretation of the verses in Daniel. See Nahmanides, *Sefer ha-Geulah* in *The Writings of Nahmanides,* Vol. 1, 287–95 and also Nahmanides' comments during the Barcelona disputation on the same issue in the same volume, 313–14.
10. *Sefer ha-Edut,* 63. *Adonai* is the way *YHWH,* the Tetragrammaton, is pronounced in Jewish circles. According to tradition, only the high priest knew the correct pronunciation of the Tetragrammaton and after the destruction of the temple, this knowledge was lost. Hence, everywhere in the Torah and liturgy that the Tetragrammaton appears, the reader pronounces it *Adonai*. One of Abulafia's central claims is that the true way of pronouncing the Tetragrammaton has been revealed to him.
11. In b.Talmud *Shabbat* 55: "the seal of God is *Emet,*" which might be the source for Abulafia's use of the word as the key to interpreting the verse

in Daniel. It is also possible that Abulafia was aware of the tradition that has in *Sefer Yetzirah* 3:2 the word *emet* rather than *emesh* thus also implying that the six rings that sealed the world were made up of the letters *aleph mem tav.* Abulafia uses the motif of seals frequently. See Y. Liebes, *Ars poetica in Sefer Yetsira* (Tel Aviv: 2000), 63–64 (n. 4, 286), 177, 185.

12. See *Sheva Netivot ha-Torah,* 103 where Abulafia shows that the name Adonai seals the power of the sun and moon when they come together every 532 years (19 x 28).

13. The twenty-eight-year solar cycle is for the calculation of Easter, which must fall on a Sunday, as once every twenty-eight years the day of the week and day of the month coincide, and the cycle can begin again. Thus, Abulafia is making his calculations based on the Easter cycle, Easter being the most important time of the year when salvation for humankind ocurred. See S. C. McClusky, *Astronomies and Cultures in Early Medieval Europe* (Cambridge: 1998), 77–96. See also R. Elior, *Temple and Chariot, Priests and Angels, Sanctuary and Heavenly Sanctuaries in Early Jewish Mysticism* (Jerusalem: 2002), 88–141 regarding the solar and lunar calendars and the intriguing issue of possible interaction with early Christianity.

14. *Sefer ha-Edut,* 64. See also *Otzar Eden Ganuz,* 274 and for the use of the verse from Isaiah in a similar manner, *Sefer ha-Heshek,* 118. In *Hayei Olam ha-Ba,* 114, written in 1280, Abulafia brings the same calculation and connects it also with the end of the reign of the seven demons which have four (7 x 4 = 28 = *koah*) faces (*panim* = 180), and 180 x 28 cycles of the sun as in the text above make the year 5040 AM (1280 AD). See also *Gan Naul,* 78–9 where again there is a similar calculation with the addition "and at the end of the exile (1280) there will be another ten years, and its [the sun's] potentiality will be completed, and its rod and the rod of its kingship will be removed from the twelve tribes of Israel."

15. The secret of *yud,* the additional ten years needed, emerges from within the word *ha-kol.* Using what is referred to as *gematria ketanah,* which is when the letters with values above ten are taken at their single digit value, *heh* = 5; *kaf* = 2; *lamed* = 3, which when added together makes ten. So *ha-kol,* which can be read as the number 5050, also has within it the secret of how that date is arrived at after the waning of the power of Christianity in 5040 (1280 AD).

16. See M. Idel, "'The Time of the End': Apocalyticism and its Spiritualization in Abraham Abulafia's Eschatology," in *Apocalyptic Time,* ed. A.

Baumgarten (Leiden: 2000), 160–63. In the same collection of essays see also O. Irshai, "Dating the Eschaton: Jewish and Christian Apocalyptic Calculation in Late Antiquity," 113–53 for the varied use of the book of Daniel.

17. *Gan Na'ul,* 79.
18. Ibid., 36–37. In *Mafteah ha-Shemot,* 10 Abulafia reiterates that the end of the exile will be in the Christian year of 1290, the acronym of *emet* and read as a number, spells out *eretz* (aleph = 1000, resh = 200, tzadi = 90). For another set of calculations that lead to 1290, see *Otzar Eden Ganuz,* 37.
19. It is interesting that each of the five books of his commentary to the Torah are referred to as keys (Key of Wisdom, Key of Names, Key to the Sacrifices, Key of the Sefirot, Key of the Sanctions) and Abulafia implies that he received the key to the text from the Divine. This is very reminiscent of Joachim's spiritual intelligence, which allowed him to develop his theory of *concordia.* See ch. 1.
20. *Mafteah ha-Hochmot,* 59–60.
21. Each letter in the Hebrew alphabet is a word in itself which, naturally, consists of letters. It is like taking the English letter B and spelling it out phonetically (bē).
22. *Mafteah ha-Hochmot,* 64.
23. *Mafteah ha-Shemot,* 130.
24. The quotation is from *Sefer Yetzirah,* 6:3 and is cited by Abulafia in *Sefer ha-Heshek,* 31. In *Ner Elohim,* 4, 69–70 one of Abulafia's disciples defines the Teli in the context of a discussion about the reasons for the Commandments. The Teli is identified with Yom Kippur (the Day of Atonement). Its head is the attribute of mercy, and the tail is the attribute of judgment. In addition, the head is identified with a positive Commandment, "I am the Lord your God," because one can have knowledge of the Divine essence through the Teli's head, and the tail is identified with a negative Commandment, "thou shall have no other gods," because it leads to false worship. In the first instance (p. 4) the head is the North Pole and is identified with God's minister, Metatron, and the tail with the South Pole, the minister of the posterior, Sandalfon.
25. *Mafteah ha-Shemot,* 106 and *Sefer ha-Heshek,* 31–33. Each constellation controls thirty degrees of the circumference, and it takes the Teli (Draco) eighteen months to go through each constellation (five degrees every three months). Also see above for the *nahash*—serpent—being a

prefiguration of Jesus. This also connects to the calculations of the end brought earlier in this chapter as being related to the waning of the power of Christianity in 1280. Compare with Revelation 12:3–4.

26. The underlying purpose of the Torah relating the story of the first redemption is "that the first redeemer wanted to convey its meaning and attributes to the last redeemer and to all who exist between the two." See *Mafteah ha-Shemot,* 109.
27. Unlike the Christian narrative, the lamb does not signify Jesus. These chapters in Exodus are at the center of Jewish-Christian polemic, for the former claim that the Messiah is still to come, and the latter interpret these verses as referring to the Crucifixion. This issue becomes particularly acute around Easter and Passover. See Yuval, *"Two Nations in Your Womb,"* 56–91.
28. That Jesus was a false god becomes clear when it is understood that the gematria of his name—*Yeshu*—is equal to *elohei nehar* (false gods = 316). See *Sitrei Torah,* 97.
29. *Mafteah ha-Shemot,* 125. The letters of the word are: *vav, heh, nun, shin, aleph, resh, yud, mem*—the *yud, shin,* and *vav* spell out Jesus, and then when the *nun,* which has a numerical value of 50, is broken down into *mem* (40) and *yud* (10), and the *heh* (5) and *aleph* (1) are added together to make *vav* (6) the remaining letters spell out *ve-Miriam* (and Miriam) the Hebrew for Mary.
30. *Mafteah ha-Shemot,* 125. In *Mafteah ha-Hochmot,* 64: "*Yom ha-Shishi* is Jesus the Nazarene, *Yom ha-Shevii* the King Messiah, half the Name in each name."
31. *Hayei ha-Olam ha-Ba,* 114.
32. Ibid., 183–84. See Idel, *Studies in Ecstatic Kabbalah,* 51–55.
33. It shows Abulafia's megalomania in thinking that he would be the one to decide on what day and date the pope would receive him.
34. *Mafteah ha-Shemot,* 130–32. On the traditions regarding the Tree of Knowledge, see R. Nelli, "La legende medievale du bois de la Croix," *Folklore* 20, no. 4 (1957): 3–12; E. O. James, "The Tree of Life," *Folklore* 79 (1968): 244–45; and Reeves, *The Figurae of Joachim of Fiore,* 24–25. See also K. Kogman-Appel, "The Tree of Death and the Tree of Life: The Hanging of Haman in Medieval Jewish Manuscript Painting," in *Between the Picture and the Word: Manuscript Studies from the Index of Christian Art,* ed. C. Hourihane (Princeton: 2005), 187–208 who discusses the inversion of Christian imagery of the Tree of Life by Jews in the thirteenth and fourteenth century.

35. Recall the Franciscan-Joachimite expectation of the Antichrist appearing in Rome in the buildup to 1290. See ch. 1.
36. Following the Hebrew dating system, the Torah commentary was written in 5049, and from what Abulafia says about two additional years, this seems to imply that he will be revealed as Messiah in 5051. See the discussion at the end of the second chapter.
37. Abulafian polemic with Christianity also extends to the Trinity and relationship between the Father and Son. In a number of places, Abulafia uses Trinitarian imagery, but emphasizes the unchanging essence of the Divine and that this supposed Trinity is a human perspective, not a Divine reality. The relevant texts are admirably translated and discussed in Wolfson, *Abraham Abulafia,* 131–33, n. 101. Abulafia is also known for his harsh critique of some of his contemporaries in that "the practitioners of sefirotic kabbalah thought to unify the Name and avoid belief in the Trinity, and they turned it into ten. And in the same manner that the gentiles [Christians] say that it is three and the three are one, so a number of these practitioners believe and say that that the Deity is ten sefirot and the ten are one . . ." See *Ve-Zot li-Yehudah* (And this is for Judah), 30.
38. See *Otzar Eden Ganuz,* 41 where Abulafia comments, "The imagination (*dimyon*) imagines, and its secret is deamon and the devil and Satan." In *Or ha-Sechel,* p. 63 Abulafia shows that *diabolus* = 359 = Satan.
39. *Mafteah ha-Shemot,* 131–35. It would be almost impossible to show here the varied techniques used by Abulafia to show how the different parts of the dreams all combine to a negative reading of Christianity, and particularly the Eucharist.
40. *Mafteah ha-Shemot,* 132–33. See also *Sefer ha-Heshek,* 83 and *Hotam ha-Haftarah,* 109.
41. In *Sefer ha-Edut,* 68 Abulafia writes: "And he said that he was in Rome at that time, and it was revealed to him what he should do and say in His name, and he should announce to all that 'the Lord reigns; let the peoples tremble' (Ps. 99:1) and the retribution is that he who crowned him will reign in his place. . . . And the matter about which it is said, 'arise and raise up the head of my messiah': this refers to the life of the souls, and the power of souls is on Rosh ha-Shana and in the temple. And he said: 'you will crown him as king': you will crown him as king from the power of all the names, for I have anointed him as king over Israel and the communities of Israel." If I

understand this passage correctly, Rosh ha-Shana brings the potential to actuality, and therefore, the importance of seeing the pope on the eve of Rosh ha-Shana in order that the true name should be proclaimed on its most efficacious day.

42. The Hebrew is very enigmatic and it is not entirely clear what Abulafia means here. Literally, it can mean that two mouths were born to him. However, if it is, perhaps, based on Judges 3:16 "*ve-lah shtei piyyot,*" referring to the sword that Ehud ben Gera, the man chosen to be Israel's deliverer, made for himself in order to kill the Moabite king, Eglon, then the meaning is slightly clearer (the Hebrew word for sword may have been accidently ommitted by a scribe who copied the manuscript). Ehud ben Gera kills the king with a two-edged sword (*herev, ve-la shtei piyyot*). Rabbi David Kimhi writes on this verse: "*ve-la shtei piyyot:* [its etymology is] from *le-fi herev* which is the sharp side of the sword. Both sides of Ehud's sword were sharp." Gersonides also comments that "the sword was made with two sharp blades (*shtei piyyot*) so that because of its sharpness it would enter easily and kill him quickly." See *Mikra'ot Gedolot (Pe'er ve-Hadar), Nevi'im* (Jerusalem: 1998). The plague is Abulafia's (the deliverer) two-edged sword, which kills the representative of the Jewish oppressors on earth.
43. Twenty-eight is *koah*—potential—and numerically equal to the name, Jesus. It is interesting in the context of the end of Christianity that Abulafia claims to have spent that amount of time with the Franciscans. Abulafia uses the verb *nitpas* a few other times in his works and it does not have a negative connotation. See for instance *Gan Naul,* 64 and *Otzar Eden Ganuz,* 61.
44. *Sefer ha-Edut,* 57–58. See H. Lenowitz, *The Jewish Messiahs: From the Galilee to Crown Heights* (Oxford: 1998), 96 who translates this passage with some mistakes, but also some interesting comments in brackets in the text.
45. The miraculous opening of prison cells is, of course, found in Acts 12:6–18, when the angel helps Peter who was incarcarated, and also in hagiographical literature. One such liberating figure is St. James, the patron saint of Spain. See Jacobus de Voragine, *The Golden Legend: Readings on the Saints,* trans. W. Granger Ryan, Vol. 2 (Princeton: 1993): 6–10.
46. See n.4 above. The Zohar text gives the actual day and date of Abulafia's attempt to see the pope. If Blickstein, *Between Philosophy*

and Mysticism, 107–23 is correct about a circle of philosophical-Kabbalists including Abulafia, Gikatilla, and Moshe de Leon, then the Zohar passage may indeed reflect direct knowledge of what happened in Rome as Moshe de Leon could have heard about it from Abulafia or Gikatilla. While, at this moment in time, Gikatilla and De Leon were moving toward theosophical Kabbalah as reflected in their later writings, they still might have remained in touch with Abulafia.

47. On the "sudden" death of Nicholas III, see A. Demski, *Papst Nicolaus III—Eine Monographie* (Munster: 1903), 347–48, who brings citations from various Christian sources.
48. See also *Sefer ha-Ot,* 67a-b: "With my **sword** I stabbed those who deny him / and His Name was the spear of my tongue / with which I killed His deniers / and I will slay his enemies with just judgement. . . . His opponent died in Rome in his rebellion / by the power of the Name of the eternal God / for YHWH fought against him both on land and on the seas." These two stanzas seem to be a reference to what happened in Rome and to the fact that the pope died by the power of Abulafia's sword, i.e., the Tetragrammaton.
49. Scholem held that Abulafia had come to speak on behalf of the Jewish nation in the same way that Moses came to Pharaoh and in accordance with what Nahmanides said in his dispute with Friar Paul in Barcelona 1263. Landauer and others felt that Abulafia's purpose was to convert Nicholas III to Judaism or to speak with the pope about Judaism. See Scholem, *Major Trends,* 128; Idel, "Abulafia and the Pope," 11–12; A. Berger, "The Messianic Self-Consciousness of Abraham Abulafia: A Tentative Evaluation," in *Essays on Jewish Life and Thought Presented in Honor of Salo Wittmayer Baron,* ed. J. L. Blau et al. (New York: 1959), 60.
50. See Idel, "Abulafia and the Pope," 13–14.
51. See the previous chapter for the etymology of the word *Yehudim.* Also see the following in *Sefer ha-Melitz,* 9, ". . . until the teaching of *yahadut* will be complete, meaning the teaching of the knowledge of the truth, and emerging from ignorance."
52. *Otzar Eden Ganuz,* 193. In the continuation of this passage, Abulafia is very critical of his contemporaries who brag about being Jewish when they do not understand what this really means. For more on this issue, see the previous chapter.
53. *Sefer ha-Edut,* 61–62.

54. Ibid., 68–69, 70,74, 75,77.
55. *Sefer ha-Haim,* 79. That this was the most important of his books is mentioned repeatedly in the other commentaries on the prophetic works, for instance: "And I will put it as the image of a seal for all the commentary which includes all the books" (*Metzaref ha-Sechel,* 7), or, "for the content of *Haftarah* is for an additional purpose as the image of a seal for the six books, but it is not a seal for the last one only, but for each and every one of them" (*Sefer ha-Yashar,* 95). *Sefer ha-Haim* is also full of self-reflective messianic statements.
56. *Hotam ha-Haftarah,* 110.
57. Ibid., 108.
58. *Sefer ha-Haftarah,* 113.
59. Joshua 10:12f and 2 Samuel 1:19–27.
60. See Patai, *The Messiah Texts,* pp. 136–37, who translates from *Midrash Zuta on Song of Songs* 5:2, ed. M. Buber (Berlin: 1894).
61. See *Sefer ha-Brit* in *Metzaref ha-Sechel,* 53–56.
62. See also Idel, *Messianic Mystics,* 306–307.
63. These books, which Abulafia took to Rome in 1280, presented, in essence, a new spiritual understanding of scriptures, and as such, intersected and overlapped with the interests of at least some of the Franciscans in Rome at this time.
64. The numerical value of Melitz is Sinim which is one of Abulafia's names for Messina. See *Sefer ha-Melitz,* 25. The prophetic work itself was written in 1281 as can be seen from parts of the original text that appear in the commentary. Abulafia talks about "the first year of kingship" hinting at "the kingdom that was once very strong and now is strengthless and very weak." *Sefer ha-Melitz,* 9. That the commentary was written in 1283 can be gleaned from a number of references to the fact that there are seven years to go, and that thirteen years have passed and we are waiting for the completion of twenty years, which points to the period from 1270–1290. Abulafia also indicated that five years hence will be the year 5048 (1288). See *Sefer ha-Melitz,* 17.
65. *Sefer ha-Melitz,* 19. However, see Wolfson, *Abraham Abulafia,* 91, who claims that the interior personal redemption through mystical experience is emphasized more than the historical dimension.
66. *Sefer ha-Melitz,* 9–21.

Chapter 5. Abulafia the "Diplomat"

1. Aescoli, *Jewish Messianic Movements,* 357–60. See also M. Eliav Feldon, "Invented Identities: Credulity in the Age of Prophecy and Exploration," *Journal of Early Modern History* 3, no. 3 (1999): 203–32.
2. On Molcho, see Idel, *Messianic Mystics,* 144–52.
3. See Adso's *Letter on the Antichrist,* in B. McGinn, *Visions of the End,* 84–85. See also R. K. Emmerson, *Antichrist in the Middle Ages: A Study of Medieval Apocalypticism, Art and Literature* (Seattle: 1981), 79–83.
4. *Calendar of the Plea Rolls of the Exchequer of the Jews,* 3 vols. (London: 1905–1929), 3:311–12. See also L. Patterson, "'The Living Witness of our Redemption': Martyrdom and Imitation in Chaucer's Prioress's Tale," *Journal of Medieval and Early Modern Studies* 31, no. 3 (2001): 542.
5. Abulafia had made no secret of his ultimate purpose and the Jews already wary of calling attention to themselves were surely horrified at the thought of Abulafia attempting to meet with the pope in the prevailing conditions and the likely consequences that this might have on the already fragile relationship with the Church. In 1270 there were attempts to confiscate Hebrew books, especially the Talmud, and in the 1280s the situation got worse, and there is enough evidence to suggest that in 1292–1293, in almost all the Apulian communities and Naples, there were mass conversions. See M. D. Cassutto, "The Destruction of the Yeshivot in Southern Italy in the Thirteenth Century" (Hebrew), in *Studies in Memory of Asher Gulak and Samuel Klein* (Jerusalem: 1942), 139–52.
6. See Armstrong, et. al., eds., *Francis of Assisi: Early Documents,* Vol. 3, *The Prophet,* 762–64.
7. See *Chronica XXIV Generalium Ordinis Fratrum Minorum,* in *Analecta Franciscana* 3 (1897), 367–69, 371.
8. Salimbene, *Chronicle,* 301–303.
9. Ibid., 304.
10. Ibid., 558.
11. The real tensions seem to begin after 1274, particularly in the March of Ancona, and in the 1290s become much more pronounced. See D. Burr, *Olivi and Franciscan Poverty: The Origins of the Usus Pauper Controversy* (Philadelphia: 1989), 1–30 and his *The Spiritual Franciscans: From Protest to Persecution in the Century after Saint Francis* (Philadelphia: 2001), 1–65.

12. See O. Schwartz and R. Lerner, "Illuminated Propaganda: The Origins of the 'Ascende calve' pope prophecies," *Journal of Medieval History* 20 (1994): 157–91 and H. Millet and D. Rigaux, "Aux origines du succès des *Vaticinia de summis pontificibus*," *Cahiers de Fanjeaux* 27 (1992): 129–56.
13. Ubertino de Casale, *The Tree of the Crucified Life of Jesus*, 179. See also N. Havely, *Dante and the Franciscans: Poverty and the Papacy in the "Commedia,"* (Cambridge: 2004), 41, 79.
14. A. Franchi, "Girolamo d'Ascoli: Origini e formazione culturale e religiosa," in E. Menestò, *Niccolò IV: Un pontificato tra oriente ed occidente* (Spoleto: 1991), 33–4.
15. See D. Flood, "Poverty as Virtue, Poverty as Warning, and Peter of John Olivi," in *Pierre de Jean Olivi (1248–1298): Pensée scolastique, dissidence spirituelle et société*, ed. A. Boureau and S. Piron (Paris: 1999), 165–66.
16. For the life of Giovanni Gaetani Orsini (Nicholas III), see Demski, *Papst Nikolaus III* and H. K. Mann and J. Hollnsteiner, *The Lives of the Popes in the Middle Ages*, Vol. 16 (London: 1932), 57–166.
17. See Lambert, *Franciscan Poverty*, 141–48 and J. Moorman, *A History of the Franciscan Order from its Origin to the Year 1517* (Oxford: 1968), 177–81.
18. Angelo Clareno has him burning Olivi's treatise on the Virgin, but when pope speaking with some warmth about Olivi, while Ubertino of Casale is mainly supportive. See Angelo Clareno, *A Chronicle or History of the Seven Tribulations of the Order of Brothers Minor*, trans. D. Burr and E. R. Daniel (North Bergen, NJ: 2005), 129–30.
19. E. Pásztor, "Girolamo d'Ascoli e Pietro di Giovanni Olivi," in E. Menestò, *Niccolò IV: Un pontificato tra oriente ed occidente* (Spoleto: 1991), 53–72 and A. Franchi, *Nicolaus Papa IV 1288–1292 (Girolamo d'Ascoli)* (Ascoli: 1990), 58. However, Jerome also condemned the works of Roger Bacon.
20. See D. Flood, *Peter Olivi's Rule Commentary* (Wiesbaden: 1972), 159.
21. See D. Burr, *Olivi and Franciscan Poverty*, 43.
22. See D. Burr, *The Persecution of Peter Olivi* (Philadelphia: 1976), 35–37. Yet, for a different reading of events see Pásztor, "Girolamo d'Ascoli e Pietro di Giovanni Olivi," 62–64.
23. See R. Lerner, "Peter Olivi on the Conversion of the Jews," in *Pierre de Jean Olivi*, 210–13 and Lerner, *Feast of St. Abraham*, 58–66. See also D. Burr, 'The Antichrist and the Jews in Four Thirteenth-Century Apocalypse Commentaries," in *Friars and Jews in the Middle Ages and Renaissance*, ed. S. J. McMichael and S. E. Myers, (Leiden 2004) 28–38.

24. I am reminded of the way Lerner chose to start his article on Joachim's teachings about the Antichrist: "Conversations with the Calabrian abbot Joachim of Fiore . . . had a way of turning to the imminent advent of Antichrist." I imagine that the same could be said about Olivi as well. See R. E. Lerner, "Antichrists and Antichrist in Joachim of Fiore," 553. See also Burr, *Olivi's Peaceable Kingdom*. It is of interest that Olivi's apocalyptic timetable is based in part on the twenty-two letters of the Hebrew alphabet.
25. On the theory and practice of interconnecting intellectual networks, see R. Collins, *The Sociology of Philosophies: A Global Theory of Intellectual Change* (Cambridge, MA and London: 1998).
26. *Otzar Eden Ganuz,* 368.
27. See Yeshayah ben Mali de Trani, *Piskei ha-Rid* (The Rulings of Rabbi Isaiah de Trani), ed. A. I. Wertheimer (Jerusalem: 1964). Interestingly, in chapter 62 of the collection, the collator brings together Zedekiah, the author of *Shibolei ha-Leket,* and Yeshayah, whom the former considered to be his teacher. Yeshayah tells Zedekiah the parable about the philosopher who was asked how he could know more than the giants who were his predecessors and responded that he was the dwarf sitting on their shoulders and could therefore see further. Yeshayah also wrote a commentary to the Prophetic books (edited by Wertheimer and printed in Jerusalem in 1991).
28. In *Sefer ha-Edut,* 57, Abulafia mentions that God informed him in the vision he had in Barcelona in late 1270, that he was to go to Rome. From the context, it is clear that the visit to Rome implied was that of 1280. If Abulafia had been to Rome in the meantime, surely it would have merited a mention? However, it is possible that in *Sefer ha-Edut* Abulafia wants to implicitly make the connection between the vision in 1270 and its fulfilment in the messianic act of 1280.
29. See H. Vogelstein and P. Rieger, *Geschichte der Juden in Rom,* 2 vols. (Berlin 1896), Vol. 1, 249, 267, 273, 376, 378, and the Anaw family tree on 456–57. See also H. Vogelstein, *A History of the Jews in Rome* (Philadelphia: 1940), 194–95. See also M. Idel, *R. Menahem Recanati the Kabbalist* (Hebrew) (Tel Aviv: 1998), 33–37.
30. In *Otzar Eden Ganuz,* 368 see Scholem, *The Kabbalah of Sefer ha-Temunah,* 193–94. Cited also in ch. 2, see text at n.16.
31. In this context, though not connected to Hillel directly, mention should be made of Moses ben Solomon of Salerno, who died in 1279, was the

disciple of Jacob Anatoli, and was in contact with both Dominicans and Franciscans. He consulted a Dominican, Nicholas of Giovenazzo, on Latin terms and brings his comments in his commentary on the *Guide for the Perplexed*. He also wrote a treatise entitled *Ta'anot* (Argumentations) in which he held levelheaded discussions with various Christian figures on their faith and proved the falsity of Christianity. Thus, it was not uncommon for Jews to be in touch with Christians in general and the mendicants in particular, and Abulafia is not unique in this Italian setting. See C. Sirat, *A History of Jewish Philosophy in the Middle Ages* (Cambridge: 1985), 266–67; J. Cohen, *The Friars and the Jews: The Evolution of Medieval Anti-Judaism* (Ithaca: 1982), 221–23, esp. n.56; Hames, *The Art of Conversion*, 280–81.

32. See the second letter from Hillel to Maestro Gaio where he briefly explains the different parts of *Tagmulei ha-Nefesh*. Z. H. Edelman, *Hemdah Genuzah* (Konigsberg: 1856), 18a-22b. See also Hillel ben Samuel of Verona, *Sefer Tagmule ha-Nefesh (Book of the Rewards of the Soul)*, ed. and intro. J. B. Sermoneta (Jerusalem: 1981), iv–vii. See also the introduction by M. Steinschneider to Hillel ben Samuel of Verona, *Sefer Tagmule ha-Nefesh* (Lyck: 1874), 7–15.
33. See his letter to Maestro Gaio, *Igrot Knaot*, 14a. On Hillel see I. E. Barzilay, *Between Reason and Faith: Anti-Rationalism in Italian Jewish Thought 1250–1650* (The Hague, Paris: 1967), 42–57. See also G. Sermoneta, "Le correnti del pensiero ebraico nell' Italia medievale," in *Italia Judaica: Atti del 1 Convegno internazionali Bari 18–22 Maggio 1981* (Rome: 1983), 273–83.
34. Abulafia had originally studied the *Guide* with Hillel in Capua. See ch. 2 above. *Hayei ha-Nefesh* is the second of Abulafia's three commentaries.
35. See A. Ravitzky, *The Thought of R. Zerahiah b. Isaac b. Shealtiel Hen and the Maimonidean-Tibbonian Philosophy in the 13th Century* (in Hebrew). PhD thesis, Hebrew University. Jerusalem: 1976, 106 and Idel, *R. Abraham Abulafia's Works and Doctrines*, 40.
36. *Hemdah Genuzah*, xxvi and *Igrot Kenaot*, 14b.
37. See Zerahiah's rebuttal of Hillel position regarding the secrets of the *Guide*. Hillel understands the secrets to refer to the Divine world whereas Zerahiah says that Maimonides was referring to the natural world only. *Otzar Nehmad* 2, p. 133. See also Barzilay, *Between Reason and Faith*, 40.

38. R. Kircheim, "About Zerahiah ha-Levi ha-Sefaradi," *Ozar Nechmad* 2 (1857): 117–43; M. Steinschneider, "Outline for the Life of Zerahiah b. Shaltiel Hen," *Ozar Nechmad* 2 (1897): 229–45; and Ravitzky, *The Thought of R. Zerahiah b. Isaac b. Shealtiel Hen,* 66–107.
39. See Y. Freidman, "R. Zerahiah ben Shaltiel Hen's *Commentary on the Guide for the Perplexed*" (Hebrew), in *Memorial Volume for Ya'aqov Freidman,* ed. S. Pines (Jerusalem: 1974), 3–14.
40. Ravitzky, *The Thought of R. Zerahiah b. Isaac b. Shealtiel Hen,* 269–92.
41. See Vogelstein and Rieger, *Geschicte der Juden in Rom,* Vol. 1, 253–54. See also S. Muntner, *Accusations against Jewish Physicians in the Light of Medical History* (in Hebrew) (Jerusalem: 1953), 10, 28; C. Roth, *A History of the Jews in Italy,* 147–49. See also I. Münz, *Die Jüdischen Aertze im Mittelalter: Ein Beitrag zur Kulturgeschichte des Mittelalters* (Frankfurt: 1922), 101–102. B. Richler, "Another Letter from Hillel ben Samuel to Isaac the Doctor?" (Hebrew), *Kiryat Sefer* 62 (1988–1989), 451 based on manuscript evidence suggests that Isaac's father was not called Mordechai.
42. M. Steinschneider, *Hebraeischen Ubersetzungen des Mittelalters* (Berlin: 1893), 670 and H. Friedenwald, *The Jews and Medicine: Essays,* 2 vols. (New York: 1944), Vol. 2, 536. Nathan de Cento was in Rome between 1279–1283 and during that period both he and Zerahiah ben Shaltiel Hen made translations of Avicenna's Canon from Arabic to Hebrew.
43. A. Lichtenberg, ed., *Kovetz Teshuvot ha-Rambam ve-Iggerotav,* III (Belfast: 1859), 13b, 14d.
44. Friedenwald, *Jews and Medicine,* Vol. 2, 560–61.
45. See M. J. Gay, *Les Registres de Nicolas III (1277–1280)* (Paris: 1898). There are letters being sent from Soriano from June 8, 1280.
46. For descriptions of the pope's sudden death, see Demski, *Papst Nikolaus III,* 348, n.1.
47. Mariano de Florentia, "Compendium Chronicorum Fr. Min. scriptum a Patre Mariano de Florentia (1181–1520)," in *Archivum franciscanum historicum* II (1909), 310: "A.D. 1249—Dominus pape in Lugdunio, de consilio Cardinalium, condonavit Fratribus Minoribus Abbatiam Sancte Maria de Araceli in Capitalio Urbis." See also Moorman, *A History of the Franciscan Order,* 119.
48. See chapter 4 of this book for the relevance of *koah.*
49. Interestingly, Abulafia ends the section describing his activities in Rome: "And I wrote these things here to extol the praises of the

Holy One Blessed be He and his wonders and signs, miracles and wondrous deeds with Raziel and his faithful servants." In other words, the whole episode from when he left Greece to his departure from Rome was considered by Abulafia to have been a series of miracles and wondrous deeds. *Sefer ha-Edut,* 58.

Conclusion

1. See the translation of the Christian version of the Barcelona disputation in H. Maccoby, *Judaism on Trial: Jewish-Christian Disputations in the Middle Ages* (London: 1993), 147. Ramon Llull, *Book of the Gentile and the Three Wise Men,* in *Selected Works of Ramon Llull,* ed. and trans. A. Bonner, 2 vols. (Princeton: 1985), Vol. 1, 149–50.
2. The medieval commentator, Rabbi Solomon Itzhaki (Rashi) starts his Torah commentary on Genesis 1 with a Midrash brought in the name of Rabbi Yitzhak to answer the question why the Torah started from Genesis and not from Exodus 12 where the first Commandments are to be found. His answer is that if the Gentiles question the Children of Israel's right to the land, they can show that God created the world and can give the land to whom he wants. See *Mikra'ot Gedolot* on Genesis 1:1. The same Midrash is also cited by Nahmanides and others.
3. *Mafteah ha-Hochmot,* 89–93.
4. Based, for example, on the first thirteen chapters of the second book of the *Liber concordia* where the different exegetical techniques are set out. This Joachite work was being studied in Southern Italy where this disputation probably took place. It is of interest that in the first chapter of this section of the book, Joachim has a Jew ask similar questions which he then answers. See Joachim of Fiore, *Liber de Concordia Novi ac Veteris Testamenti,* 53–61.
5. St. Bonaventure discourses on the meaning of the ladder in Jacob's dream in a sermon delivered in Paris 1267 to commemorate the thirty-seventh anniversary of the transferral of the body of St. Francis to the basilica in Assisi. For Bonaventure the ladder is Christ who is in heaven in His divinity and on earth in His humanity. So one, like Francis, can ascend the ladder by calling on Christ. This is not so different a reading from Abulafia's and might explain the Christian's acquiescence in Abulafia's explanation. See Armstrong et al., *Francis of Assisi: The Founder,* 744.

6. Abulafia takes the Augustinian concept of the *testimonium veritates,* which accords the Jews a special place as *capsarii* of the Torah which bears witness to Christ, and turns it on its head. The Torah is indeed a witness, but to the close relationship that has always existed and will always exist between God and Israel. See Cohen, *Living Letters of the Law,* 19–65. For Bonaventure, Jacob's ladder also represents the stages of prayer, ways of understanding scripture and progression in virtue. See Armstrong et al., *Francis of Assisi: The Founder,* 630, a.
7. Elena Lourie, in her article dealing with the Ribat as an influence on the founding of the military orders, asks: "What constitutes 'direct evidence' when discussing the problem of cultural borrowing?" In her discussion she cites M. J. Herskovits, *Cultural Anthropology* (New York: 1960), 467–68: "The similarities would have to include *similar traits, similarly related to give proof of diffusion,* and this moreover only within a restricted area where communication between borrowers and lenders was not difficult to assume." See E. Lourie, "The Confraternity of Belchite, the Ribat, and the Temple," *Viator* 13 (1982): 162–63 (Reprinted in her *Crusade and Colonisation: Muslims, Christians, and Jews in Medieval Aragon* [Aldershot: 1990], II).
8. Joachim of Fiore, *Liber Concordie Novi et Veteris Testamenti,* Book V (Venice: 1519), f. 135rb. See also McGinn, *The Calabrian Abbot,* 190.
9. Reeves, *The Figurae of Joachim of Fiore,* 41–42, n.89.

Bibliography

Primary Sources

Abulafia, Abraham. *Ve-Zot le-Yehudah* (And This Is for Judah). In A. Jellinek, *Auswahl Kabbalistischer Mystik*. Leipzig: 1853.

———. *Sheva Netivot ha-Torah* (Seven Paths of the Torah). In *Philosophie und Kabbala*, ed. A. Jellinek. Leipzig: 1854.

———. "*Sefer ha-Ot*. Apokalypse des Pseudo-Propheten und Pseudo-Messias Abraham Abulafia vollendet im Jahre 1285." In *Jubelschrift zum Siebzigsten Geburstage de Prof. Dr. H. Graetz*. Breslau: 1887.

———. *Or ha-Sechel*. Ed. M. Safrin. Jerusalem: 1999.

———. *Sefer ha-Heshek*. Ed. M. Safrin. Jerusalem: 1999.

———. *Imrei Shefer*. Ed. A. Gross. Jerusalem: 1999.

———. *Hayei ha-Olam ha-Ba*. Ed. A. Gross. Jerusalem: 1999 (*Ve-Zot le-Yehudah* is also printed in this volume).

———. *Gan Na'ul*. Ed. A. Gross. Jerusalem: 1999 (*Sheva Netivot ha-Torah* is also printed in this volume).

———. *Otzar Eden Ganuz*. Ed. A. Gross. Jerusalem: 2000.

———. *Mafteah ha-Hochmot, Mafteah ha-Shemot*. Ed. A. Gross. Jerusalem: 2001 (Abulafia's commentary to Genesis and Exodus).

———. *Mafteah ha-Sefirot, Mafteah ha-Tochehot*. Ed. A. Gross. Jerusalem: 2001 (Abulafia's commentary to Numbers and Deuteronomy).

———. *Sitrei Torah*. Ed. A. Gross. Jerusalem: 2001.

———. *Or ha-Sechel ve-Shomer Mitzvah*. Ed. A. Gross. Jerusalem: 2001.

———. *Hayei ha-Nefesh*. Ed. A. Gross. Jerusalem: 2001 (*Metzaref la-Kesef* is also printed in this volume).

———. *Metzaref ha-Sechel ve-Sefer ha-Ot*. Ed. A. Gross. Jerusalem: 2001 (includes *Sefer ha-Melitz, Sefer Ish Adam, Sefer ha-Brit, Sefer ha-Edut, Sefer ha-Haim, Sefer ha-Yashar, Sefer ha-Haftarah* and *Sefer ha-Ot*).

———. *Sefer ha-Geulah*. Ed. R. Cohen. Jerusalem: 2001.

———. *Mafteah ha-Ra'ayon, ha-Heshek ve-ha-Melamed*. Ed. A. Gross. Jerusalem 2002 (includes three books—*Mafteah ha-Ra'ayon, Sefer ha-Heshek,* and *Sefer ha-Melamed*).

———. *Ner Elohim, Get ha-Shemot.* Ed. A. Gross. Jerusalem: 2002 (*Ner Elohim* is actually a work by Abulafia's disciple, Nathan ben Sa'adyahu Harar).

Aescoli, A. Z. *Jewish Messianic Movements: Sources and Documents on Messianism in Jewish History from the Bar-Kohba Revolt until Recent Times* (Hebrew). Jerusalem: 1987. (2nd edition)

Angelo Clareno. *A Chronicle or History of the Seven Tribulations of the Order of Brothers Minor.* Trans. D. Burr and E. R. Daniel. North Bergen, NJ: 2005.

Armstrong, R. J. et al., eds. *Francis of Assisi: Early Documents* (Vol. 1: *The Saint,* Vol 2: *The Founder,* Vol 3: *The Prophet*). New York: 1999–2001.

Augustine, St. *City of God against the Pagans.* Ed. and trans. R. W. Dyson. Cambridge: 1998.

Bonaventura, *Legenda maiora.* Trans. B. Fahy. In *St. Francis of Assisi: Writings and Early Biographies,* ed. M. A. Habig. Quincy, IL: 1991.

Calendar of the Plea Rolls of the Exchequer of the Jews. 3 vols. London: 1905–1929.

Chronica XXIV Generalium Ordinis Fratrum Minorum (1209- 1374), cum pluribus Appendicibus, inter quas excellit hucusque ineditus "Liber de Laudibus S. Francisci" fr. Bernardi de Bessa. Vol. III of the *Analecta Franciscana.* Quaracchi: 1897.

Dan, J., ed. *The Heart and the Fountain: An Anthology of Jewish Mystical Experiences.* Oxford: 2002.

Filippo Cagliola. *Almae Siciliensis Provinciae Ordinis Minorum Conventualium S. Francisci.* Venice: 1644, fasc. Palermo: 1984.

Flood, D. *Peter Olivi's Rule Commentary.* Wiesbaden: 1972.

Gay, M. J. *Les Registres de Nicolas III (1277–1280).* Paris: 1898.

Goodman, L. (trans), *Ibn Tufayl's Hayy ibn Yaqzan, a Philosophical Tale* (New York: 1992).

Hillel ben Samuel of Verona. *Sefer Tagmule ha-Nefesh (Book of the Rewards of the Soul).* Ed. and Intro. J. B. Sermoneta. Jerusalem: 1981.

———. "Iggeret Rabbi Hillel Ha-Hasid el Rabbi Yitzhak ha-Rofe" (The Letter of Rabbi Hillel the Pious to Rabbi Isaac the Physician). In *Igrot Kena'ot, Kovetz Teshubot ha-Rambam ve-Iggerotav,* ed. A. Lichtenberg. Leipzig: 1859.

Jacobs, L. *The Schoken Book of Jewish Mystical Testimonies.* New York: 1997.

Jacobus de Voragine. *The Golden Legend: Readings on the Saints.* Trans. W. Granger Ryan. 2 vols. Princeton: 1993.

Joachim of Fiore. *Adversus Judaeos.* Ed. A. Frugoni. Rome: 1957.

———. *Enchiridion super Apocalypsim*. Ed. E. K. Burger. Toronto: 1986.

———. *Exposito in Apocalypsim*. Venice: 1527.

———. *Praephatio super Apocalypsim*. Ed. K-V. Selge, with Italian translation in Gioacchino da Fiore, *Introduzione all'Apocalisse*. Rome: 1995.

———. *Liber Concordie Novi et Veteris Testamenti*. Venice: 1519.

———. *Liber de Concordia Novi ac Veteris Testamenti*. Ed. E. R. Daniel. *Transactions of the American Philosophical Society*, 73. Philadelphia: 1983 (the first four books).

———. *Liber figurarum*. Ms. Oxford, Corpus Christi College, 255A, ff. 4v–17v.

———. *Psalterium Decem Chordarum*. Ed. and trans. E. Russo. Chiaravalle Centrale: 1983.

———. *Tractatus super Quatuor Evangelia*. Ed. E. Buonaiutu. Rome: 1930. Translated into Italian as Gioacchino da Fiore, *Trattati sui quattro Vangeli*. Trans. L. Pellegrini. Rome: 1999.

———. (Pseudo). *Epistola subsequentium figurarum*, Ms. Vatican Lat. 3822.

———. (Pseudo). *Super Hieremiam Prophetam*. Venice: 1516.

———. (Pseudo). *Super Esaiam Prophetam*. Venice: 1517 (preceded by the *Praemissiones*).

Joseph Gikatilla. *Sha'are Orah*. Ed. J. Ben Shlomo, 2 vols. Jerusalem: 1981.

Judah the Pious. *Sefer Gematriot of R. Judah the Pious*. Intros. D. Abrams and I. Ta-Shma. Los Angeles: 1998.

Kaplan, A. *Meditation and Kabbalah*. Northvale, N. J.: 1995.

Lichtenberg, A., ed. *Kovetz Teshuvot ha-Rambam ve-Iggerotav*, III. Belfast: 1859.

Limor, O., ed. *Die Disputationen zu Ceuta (1179) und zu Mallorca (1286): zwei antijudische Schriften aus dem mittelalterlichen Genua*. Munich: 1994.

Luard, H. R., ed. *Matthaei Parisiensis Monachi Sancti Albani Chronica Maiora* (Rolls Series 57), 7 vols. London: 1872–83.

Mariano de Florentia. "Compendium Chronicorum Fr. Min. scriptum a Patre Mariano de Florentia (1181–1520)." In *Archivum franciscanum historicum* I. 1908. 98–107; II. 1909. 92–107; 305–318; 457–72; 626–41.

McGinn, B. *Apocalyptic Spirituality: Treatises and Letters of Laetantius, Adso of Montier-en-Der, Joachim of Fiore, The Spiritual Franciscans, Savonarola* (Mahwah, New Jersey: 1979)

———. *Visions of the End: Apocalyptic Traditions in the Middle Ages*. New York: 1998.

Midrash Zuta on Song of Songs. Ed. M. Buber. Berlin: 1894.

Nahmanides. *The Writings of Nahmanides.* Ed. C. D. Chavel. 2 vols. Jerusalem: 1963.

———. *Torah Commentary.* Ed. C. D. Chavel. 2 vols. Jerusalem: 1959.

Ramon Llull. *Book of the Gentile and the Three Wise Men.* In *Selected Works of Ramon Llull,* ed. and trans. A. Bonner. 2 vols. Princeton: 1985.

Salimbene de Adam. *The Chronicle of Salimbene de Adam.* Trans. J. L. Baird. New York: 1986.

Solomon ibn Adret. *Responsa.* Ed. H. Dimitrovsky. 2 vols. Jerusalem: 1990.

Ubertino de Casale, *The Tree of the Crucified Life of Jesus.* In *Francis of Assisi: Early Documents—The Prophet,* ed. R. J. Armstrong et al. New York: 2001.

Yeshayah ben Mali de Trani, *Piskei ha-Rid* (The Rulings of Rabbi Isaiah de Trani), ed. A. I. Wertheimer. Jerusalem: 1964.

Zohar (with Hebrew translation). 10 Vols. Jerusalem: 1998.

Secondary Sources

Abrams, D. *Sexual Symbolism and the Account of the Chariot in Medieval Germany: A Study of the Sod ha-Egoz Texts.* Tübingen: 1997.

Abulafia, D. *Frederick II: A Medieval Emperor.* London: 1988.

———. *The Western Mediterranean Kingdoms 1200–1500.* London and New York: 1997.

———. "The Kingdom of Sicily under the Hohenstaufen and Angevins." In *The New Cambridge Medieval History,* Vol. 5, *c. 1198-c. 1300,* ed. D. Abulafia. Cambridge: 1999.

Altmann, A. "Maimonides's Attitude Toward Jewish Mysticism." In *Studies in Jewish Thought: An Anthology of German Jewish Scholarship,* ed. A. Jospe. Detroit: 1981.

Assis, Y. T. *The Golden Age of Aragonese Jewry: Community and Society in the Crown of Aragon, 1213–1327.* London: 1997.

Backman, C. R. "Arnau de Villanova and the Franciscan Spirituals in Sicily." *Franciscan Studies* 50 (1990): 1–29.

Baer, Y. *A History of the Jews in Christian Spain.* 2 vols. Philadelphia: 1992.

Baraut, C. "Las antiguas biografias de Joaquín de Fiore y sus fuentes." *Analecta Sacra Tarraconensia* 26 (1953): 207–25.

Barber, M. *The Two Cities: Medieval Europe 1050–1320.* London and New York: 1992.

Barzilay, I. E. *Between Reason and Faith: Anti-Rationalism in Italian Jewish Thought 1250–1650*. The Hague, Paris: 1967.

Benjamin, S. *The World of Benjamin of Tudela: A Medieval Mediterranean Travelogue*. London: 1995.

Bensch, S. P. *Barcelona and its Rulers, 1096–1291*. Cambridge: 1995.

Berger, A. "The Messianic Self-Consciousness of Abraham Abulafia: A Tentative Evaluation." In *Essays on Jewish Life and Thought Presented in Honor of Salo Wittmayer Baron*, ed. J. L. Blau et al. New York: 1959.

———. "Captive at the Gate of Rome: The Story of a Messianic Motif." *Proceedings of the American Academy for Jewish Research* 44 (1977): 1–17.

Berner, L. *On the Western Shores: The Jews of Barcelona during the Reign of Jaume I, "el Conqueridor," 1213–1276*. PhD Dissertation. UCLA. Los Angeles: 1986.

Biale, D. *Gerschom Scholem: Kabbalah and Counter-History*. Cambridge, MA: 1982.

Blank, A. "Trinität und Geschichte in Joachim von Fiores *Psalterium decem chordarum*." *Florensia* 10 (1996): 155–70.

Blickstein, S. *Between Philosophy and Mysticism: A Study of the Philosophical-Qabbalistic Writings of Joseph Giqatila (1248-c. 1322)*. PhD Dissertation. Jewish Theological Seminary. New York: 1983.

Bokser, B. *The Jewish Mystical Tradition*. Northvale, NJ: 1993.

Burr, D. *The Persecution of Peter Olivi*. Philadelphia: 1976.

———. *Olivi and Franciscan Poverty: The Origins of the Usus Pauper Controversy*. Philadelphia; 1989.

———. *Olivi's Peaceable Kingdom: A Reading of the Apocalypse Commentary*. Philadelphia: 1993.

———. *The Spiritual Franciscans: From Protest to Persecution in the Century after Saint Francis*. University Park, PA: 2001.

———. 'The Antichrist and the Jews in Four Thirteenth-Century commentaries," in *Friars and Jews in the Middle Ages and Renaissance*, ed. S. J. McMichael and S. E. Myers, Leiden: 2004.

Capelli, A. *Cronologia, Cronographia, e Calendrio Perpetuo*. Milan: 1988.

Cassuto, U. 'The Extinction of the South-Italian Academies in the Thirteenth Century" (Hebrew). In *Studies in Memory of Asher Gulak and Samuel Klein*. Jerusalem: 1942.

Cassutto, M. D. "The Destruction of the Yeshivot in Southern Italy in the Thirteenth Century" (Hebrew). In *Studies in Memory of Asher Gulak and Samuel Klein*. Jerusalem: 1942.

Cohen, J. *The Friars and the Jews: The Evolution of Medieval Anti-Judaism.* Ithaca: 1982.

———. *Living Letters of the Law: Ideas of the Jew in Medieval Christianity.* Berkeley: 1999.

———. "*Synagoga Conversa:* Honorius Augustodunensis, the Song of Songs, and Christianity's 'Eschatological Jew.'" *Speculum* 79 (2004): 309–40.

Cohn, N. *The Pursuit of the Millenium: Revolutionary Millenarians and Mystical Anarchists of the Middle Ages.* London: 1970.

Collins, R. *The Sociology of Philosophies: A Global Theory of Intellectual Change.* Cambridge, MA and London: 1998.

Dan, J. *Hasidism in Medieval Germany* (Hebrew). Tel Aviv: 1992.

Daniel, E. R. "A Re-examination of the Origins of Franciscan Joachitism." *Speculum* 43 (1968): 671–76.

———. "Apocalyptic Conversion: The Joachite Alternative to the Crusades," *Traditio* 25 (1969): 128–54.

———. *The Franciscan Concept of Mission in the High Middle Ages.* Lexington: 1975.

———. "Abbot Joachim of Fiore and the Conversion of the Jews." In *Friars and Jews in the Middle Ages and Renaissance,* ed. S. J. McMichael and S. E. Myers. Leiden: 2004.

Demski, A. *Papst Nicolaus III—Eine Monographie.* Munster: 1903.

Denifle, H. "Das Evangelium acturnum und die Commission eu Prasni" *Archivsür Literatur und Kirchengeschicchte des Mittelalters,* 1 (1885): 49–142.

Douie, D. L. *The Nature and the Effect of the Heresy of the Fraticelli.* Manchester: 1932.

Eco, U. *The Search for the Perfect Language.* Oxford: 1995.

Edelman, Z. H. *Hemdah Genuzah.* Konigsberg: 1856.

Elbogen, I. *Jewish Prayer in its Historical Development* (Hebrew). Tel Aviv: 1972.

Eliav Feldon, M. "Invented Identities: Credulity in the Age of Prophecy and Exploration." *Journal of Early Modern History* 3, no. 3 (1999): 203–32.

Elior, R. *Temple and Chariot, Priests and Angels, Sanctuary and Heavenly Sanctuaries in Early Jewish Mysticism* (Hebrew). Jerusalem: 2002.

Epstein, A. "The Story of Eldan ha-Deni." In *The Writings of Abraham Epstein,* Vol. 1, ed. A. M. Haberman. Jerusalem: 1950.

Flood, D. "Poverty as Virtue, Poverty as Warning, and Peter of John Olivi." In *Pierre de Jean Olivi (1248–1298): Pensée scolastique, dissidence spirituelle et société,* ed. A. Boureau and S. Piron. Paris: 1999.

Franchi, A. *Nicolaus Papa IV 1288–1292 (Girolamo d'Ascoli)*. Ascoli: 1990.

———. "Girolamo d'Ascoli: Origini e formazione culturale e religiosa." In E. Menestò, *Niccolò IV: Un pontificato tra oriente ed occidente*. Spoleto: 1991.

Freidman, Y. "R. Zerahiah ben Shaltiel Hen's *Commentary on the Guide for the Perplexed*" (Hebrew). In *Memorial Volume for Ya'aqov Freidman*, ed. S. Pines. Jerusalem: 1974.

Freller, T. "A German Clergyman in Medieval Malta: The Famous Itinerary of Ludolph von Suchen and the Maltese Islands." *European Journal of Theology* 5, no. 1 (1996): 15–26.

Friedenwald, H. *The Jews and Medicine: Essays*. 2 vols. New York: 1944.

Funkenstein, A. *Perceptions of Jewish History*. Berkeley: 1993.

Gil, M. "The Jews in Sicily under Muslim Rule in the Light of the Geniza Documents." In *Italia judaica: Atti del I convegno internazionale, Bari 18–22 Maggio 1981*. Rome: 1983.

Ginsburg, C. D. *The Kabbalah: Its Doctrines, Development, and Literature*. London: 1920.

Goldish, M. *The Sabbatean Prophets*. Cambridge, MA: 2004.

Gow, A. *The Red Jews: Antisemitism in an Apocalyptic Age*. Leiden: 1995.

Graetz, H. "Abraham Abulafia, der Pseudomessias." *Monatsschrift für Geschichte und Wissenschaft des Judentums* 36 (1887): 557–58.

Grundmann, H. "Zur Biographie Joachims von Fiore und Rainers von Ponza." *Deutsches Archiv für Erforschung des Mittelalters* 16 (1960): 437–564.

———. *Ausgewählte Aufsästze*, vol. 2, *Joachim von Fiore*. Stuttgart: 1977.

Halbertal, M. *By Way of Truth: Nahmanides and the Creation of Tradition* (Hebrew). Jerusalem: 2006.

Hames, H. J. *The Art of Conversion: Christianity and Kabbalah in the Thirteenth Century*. Leiden: 2000.

———. "From Calabria Cometh the Law, and the Word of the Lord from Sicily: The Holy Land in the Thought of Joachim of Fiore and Abraham Abulafia." *Mediterranean Historical Review* 20, no. 2 (2005): 187–99.

———. "A Seal within a Seal: The Imprint of Sufism in Abraham Abulafia's Teachings." *Medieval Encounters* 11, no. 4 (2006): 153–72.

———. "Three in One or One that is Three: On the Dating of Abraham Abulafia's *Sefer ha-Ot*." *Revue des Etudes Juives* 165, no. 1–2 (2006): 179–89.

Havely, N. *Dante and the Franciscans: Poverty and the Papacy in the "Commedia."* Cambridge: 2004.

Henoch, C. *Nahmanides: Philosopher and Mystic.* Jerusalem: 1978.

Hillenbrand, C. *The Crusades: Islamic Perspectives.* Edinburgh: 1999.

Hillgarth, J. N. *The Spanish Kingdoms 1210–1516,* 2 vols. Oxford: 1976–1978.

Hirsch-Reich, B. "Joachim von Fiore und das Judentum." In *Judentum im Mittelalter,* ed. P. Wilpert and P. Eckert. Berlin: 1966.

Idel, M. *Abraham Abulafia's Works and Doctrines.* PhD thesis, Hebrew University, Jerusalem, 1976.

———. "Abraham Abulafia and the Pope: The Meaning and Metamorphosis of an Abortive Attempt" (Hebrew). *Association of Jewish Studies Review* 7–8 (1982–1983): 1–17.

———. "La història de la Càbala a Barcelona." *Curs la Càbala.* Barcelona: 1985.

———. *Kabbalah: New Perspectives.* New Haven and London: 1988.

———. *Studies in Ecstatic Kabbalah.* Albany: 1988.

———. *The Mystical Experience in Abraham Abulafia.* Jerusalem: 1988.

———. *Language, Torah, and Hermeneutics in Abraham Abulafia.* Albany: 1989.

———. "The Contribution of Abraham Abulafia's Kabbalah to the Understanding of Jewish Mysticism." In *Gershom Scholem's Major Trends in Jewish Mysticism 50 Years After,* ed. Schäfer and Dan. Tübingen: 1993.

———. *Hasidism: Between Ecstasy and Magic.* New York: 1995.

———. "Abulafia's Secrets of the Guide: A Linguistic Turn." In *Perspectives on Jewish Thought and Mysticism,* ed. A. L. Ivry, E. R. Wolfson, and A. Arkush. Amsterdam: 1998.

———. "Nahmanides: Kabbalah, Halakhah, and Spiritual Leadership." In M. Idel and M. Ostrow, *Jewish Mystical Leaders and Leadership in the 13th Century.* Northvale, NJ: 1998.

———. *Messianic Mystics.* New Haven and London: 1998.

———. *R. Menahem Recanati the Kabbalist* (Hebrew). Tel Aviv: 1998.

———. "The Rashba and Abraham Abulafia: The Story of an Ignored Kabbalistic Polemic" (Hebrew). In *Atara l'Haim: Studies in the Talmud and Medieval Rabbinic Literature in Honor of Professor Haim Zalman Dimitrovsky,* ed. D. Boyarin et al. Jerusalem: 2000.

———. "'The Time of the End': Apocalyticism and its Spiritualization in Abraham Abulafia's Eschatology." In *Apocalyptic Time,* ed. A. Baumgarten. Leiden: 2000.

———. "Abraham Abulafia and Menahem ben Benjamin in Rome: The Beginnings of Kabbalah in Italy." In *The Jews of Italy: Memory and Identity,* ed. B. D. Cooperman and B. Garvin. Bethesda: 2000.

———. *Absorbing Perfections: Kabbalah and Interpretations.* New Haven and London: 2002.

———. "Rabbi Nathan ben Sa'adiah Harar, Author of *Sha'arei Tzedek* and His Influence in the Land of Israel" (Hebrew). *Shalem* 7 (2002): 47–58.

———. "Maimonides' *Guide for the Perplexed* and the Kabbalah." *Jewish History* 18, no. 2–3 (2004): 206–209.

———. "From Italy to Ashkenaz and Back: On the Circulation of Jewish Mystical Traditions," *Kabbalah* 14, (2006) 47–94.

Irshai, O. "Dating the Eschaton: Jewish and Christian Apocalyptic Calculation in Late Antiquity." In *Apocalyptic Time,* ed. A. Baumgarten. Leiden: 2000.

James, E. O. "The Tree of Life," *Folklore* 79 (1968): 241–49.

Keiner, R. "From *Ba'al ha-Zohar* to Prophet to Ecstatic: The Vicissitudes of Abulafia in Contemporary Scholarship." In *Gershom Scholem's Major Trends in Jewish Mysticism 50 Years After,* ed. P. Schäfer and J. Dan. Tübingen: 1993.

Kircheim, R. "About Zerahiah ha-Levi ha-Sefaradi" (Hebrew). *Ozar Nechmad* 2 (1857): 117–43.

Klein, E. *Jews, Christian Society, and Royal Power in Medieval Barcelona.* Ann Arbor: 2006.

Knohel, I. "On the 'Son of God,' Armilus and the Messiah son of Joseph" (Hebrew). *Tarbiz* 58 (1998): 13–37.

———. *The Messiah before Jesus* (Hebrew). Tel Aviv: 2000.

Kogman-Appel, K. "The Tree of Death and the Tree of Life: The Hanging of Haman in Medieval Jewish Manuscript Painting," in *Between the Picture and the Word: Manuscript Studies from the Index of Christian Art,* ed. C. Hourihane. Princeton: 2005.

Lambert, M. D. *Franciscan Poverty: The Doctrine of Absolute Poverty of Christ and the Apostles in the Franciscan Order 1210–1323.* New York: 1982.

Landauer, M. *Literaturblatt des Orients* 6 (1845), 380–83, 417–22, 471–75, 488–92, 507–10, 525–28, 556–58, 570–74, 588–92, 747–50.

Lenowitz, H. *The Jewish Messiahs: From the Galilee to Crown Heights.* Oxford: 1998.

Lerner, R. E. "Antichrists and Antichrist in Joachim of Fiore." *Speculum* 60, no. 3 (1985): 553–70.

———. "Frederick II, Alive, Aloft, and Allayed, in Franciscan-Joachite Eschatology." In *The Use and Abuse of Eschatology In the Middle Ages,* ed. W. Verbeke et al. Leuven: 1988.

———. "Peter Olivi on the Conversion of the Jews." In *Pierre de Jean Olivi (1248–1298): Pensée scolastique, dissidence spirituelle et société*. Paris: 1999.

———. *The Feast of St. Abraham: Medieval Millenarians and the Jews.* Philadelphia: 2001.

Liebes, Y. *Ars poetica in Sefer Yetsira* (Hebrew). Tel Aviv: 2000.

Lipton, S. *Images of Intolerance: The Representation of Jews and Judaism in the Bible moralisée.* Berkeley, Los Angeles, London: 1999.

Lourie, E. "The Confraternity of Belchite, the Ribat, and the Temple." *Viator* 13 (1982): 162–63 (Reprinted in E. Lourie. *Crusade and Colonisation: Muslims, Christians, and Jews in Medieval Aragon*. Aldershot: 1990).

Luca Potesta G. *Il Tempo dell'Apocalypse: Vita di Gioacchino da Fiore.* Rome and Bari: 2004.

Maccoby, H. *Judaism on Trial: Jewish-Christian Disputations in the Middle Ages.* London: 1993.

Mann, H. K., and J. Hollnsteiner. *The Lives of the Popes in the Middle Ages.* Vol 16. London: 1932.

Marcus, I. *Piety and Society: The Jewish Pietists of Medieval Germany.* Leiden: 1981.

McClusky, S. C. *Astronomies and Cultures in Early Medieval Europe.* Cambridge: 1998.

McGinn, B. *The Calabrian Abbot: Joachim of Fiore in the History of Western Thought.* New York and London: 1985.

———. "Angel Pope and Papal Antichrist." In *Apocalypticism in the Western Tradition*. Aldershot: 1994.

———. "Apocalyptic Traditions and Spiritual Identity in Thirteenth-Century Religious Life." In *Apocalypticism in the Western Tradition*. Aldershot: 1994.

Millet, H., and D. Rigaux. "Aux origines du succès des *Vaticinia de summis pontificibus*." *Cahiers de Fanjeaux* 27 (1992): 129–56.

Moorman, J. *A History of the Franciscan Order from its Origin to the Year 1517.* Oxford: 1968.

Moynihan, R. "The Development of the 'Pseudo-Joachim' Commentary 'Super Hieremiam': New Manuscript Evidence." *Mélanges de l'Ecole Française de Rome, Moyen âge—Temps modernes* 98 (1986): 109–42.

Muntner, S. *Accusations against Jewish Physicians in the Light of Medical History* (Hebrew). Jerusalem: 1953.

Münz, I. *Die Jüdischen Aertze im Mittelalter: Ein Beitrag zur Kulturgeschichte des Mittelalters.* Frankfurt: 1922.

Nelli, R. "La legende medievale du bois de la Croix." *Folklore* 20, no. 4 (1957): 3–12.

Neubauer, A. "Where are the Ten Tribes?" *Jewish Quarterly Review* 1 (1888–89): 14–28, 95–114, 185–201, 408–23.

Neuman, A. *The Jews in Spain*. 2 Vols. Philadelphia: 1969.

Oliverio, S. "*Vita beati Joachimi Abbatis.*" *Florensia* 16–17 (2002–2003): 220–40.

Pásztor, E. "Girolamo d'Ascoli e Pietro di Giovanni Olivi." In E. Menestò, *Niccolò IV: Un pontificato tra oriente ed occidente*. Spoleto: 1991.

Patai, R. *The Messiah Texts*. Detroit: 1988.

Patchovsky, A. *Dei Bildwelt der Diagramme Joachims von Fiore: Zur Medialität religiös—politischer Programme im Mittelalter.* Berlin: 2003.

Patterson, L. "'The Living Witness of our Redemption': Martyrdom and Imitation in Chaucer's Prioress's Tale." *Journal of Medieval and Early Modern Studies* 31, no. 3 (2001): 507–60.

Pedaya, H. *Vision and Speech: Models of Revelatory Experience in Jewish Mysticism*. Los Angeles: 2002.

———. *Nahmanides: Cyclical Time and Holy Text* (Hebrew). Tel Aviv: 2003.

Pick, B. *The Cabala: Its Influence on Judaism and Christianity.* Chicago: 1913(?).

Pou y Martí, J. *Visionarios, Beguinos, y Fraticelos Catalanes (siglos XIII–XV).* Intro. A. Hauf i Valls. Alicante: 1996.

Prawer, J. *The History of the Jews in the Latin Kingdom of Jerusalem*. Jerusalem: 2000.

Ratzinger, J. *The Theology of History in St. Bonaventure.* Chicago: 1989.

Ravitzky, A. *The Thought of R. Zerahiah b. Isaac b. Shealtiel Hen and the Maimonidean-Tibbonian Philosophy in the 13th Century* (Hebrew), PhD thesis, Hebrew University (Jerusalem: 1976).

Reeves, M. "The *Liber Figurarum* of Joachim of Fiore." *Mediaeval and Renaissance Studies* 2 (1950): 57–81.

———. "The Abbot Joachim's Disciples and the Cistercian Order." *Sophia* 19 (1951): 355–71.

———. and B. Hirsch-Reich. "The *Figurae* of Joachim of Fiore: Genuine and Spurious Collections." *Medieval and Renaissance Studies* 3 (1954): 170–99.

———. and B. Hirsch-Reich. *The Figurae of Joachim of Fiore.* Oxford: 1972.

———. *The Influence of Prophecy in the Later Middle Ages: A Study in Joachimism.* Notre Dame: 1993.

———. *Joachim of Fiore and the Prophetic Future: A Medieval Study in Historical Thinking.* Stroud: 1999.

Richler, B. "Another Letter from Hillel ben Samuel to Isaac the Doctor?" (Hebrew). *Kiryat Sefer* 62 (1988–1989): 450–52.

Riedl, M. *Joachim von Fiore: Deaker der Vollerveter Menschheit.* Wurzburg: 2004.

Robb, F. "Did Innocent III Personally Condemn Joachim of Fiore?" *Florensia* 7 (1993): 82–87.

———. "The Fourth Lateran Council's Definition of Trinitarian Orthodoxy." *Journal of Ecclesiastical History* 48 (1997): 22–43.

Roth, C. *The History of the Jews in Italy.* Philadelphia: 1946.

Runciman, S. *The Sicilian Vespers: A History of the Mediterranean World in the Later Thirteenth Century.* Cambridge: 1958.

Sapir Abulafia, A. "The Conquest of Jerusalem: Joachim of Fiore and the Jews." In *The Experience of Crusading,* Vol. 1, *Western Approaches,* ed. M. Bull and N. Housley. Cambridge: 2003.

Sarachek, J. *Faith and Reason: The Conflict over the Rationalism of Maimonides.* Williamsport: 1935.

Schmeider, F. 'Nota sectan macmeticam alterendam a tartaris et christianis:' The Mongols as non-believing apocalyptic friends around the year 1260,' *Journal of Millenial Studies* 1:1 (1998) 1–11.

Scholem, G. *Major Trends in Jewish Mysticism.* Jerusalem: 1941.

———. *On the Kabbalah and Its Symbolism.* New York: 1965.

———. *The Messianic Idea in Judaism and other Essays on Jewish Spirituality.* New York: 1971.

———. "The Name of God and the Linguistic Theory of the Kabbala." *Diogenes* 79 (1972): 59–80 and *Diogenes* 80 (1972): 164–94.

———. *The Kabbalah of Sefer ha-Temunah and Abraham Abulafia.* Ed. I. Ben Shelomo. Jerusalem: 1987.

———. *Origins of the Kabbalah.* Princeton: 1990.

Schwartz, O., and R. Lerner. "Illuminated Propaganda: The Origins of the 'Ascende calve' pope prophecies." *Journal of Medieval History* 20 (1994): 157–91.

Schwartz, Y. 'Magic, Philosophy and Kabbalah: The Mystical and Magical Interpretation of Maimonides in the Later Middle Ages (Hebrew),' Da'at (forthcoming 2007).

Sermoneta, G. "Le correnti del pensiero ebraico nell' Italia medievale." In *Italia Judaica: Atti del 1 Convegno internazionali Bari 18–22 Maggio 1981.* Rome: 1983.

Sermoneta, J. B. "Thine Ointments Have a Goodly Fragrance: Rabbi Judah Romano and the Open Text Method" (Hebrew). In *Shlomo*

Pines Jubilee Volume, Vol. 2, ed. M. Idel, W. Z. Harvey, E. Schweid. Jerusalem: 1990.

Shagrir, I. "The Parable of the Three Rings: A Revision of its History." *Journal of Medieval History* 23, no. 2 (1997): 163–77.

Shalev-Eyni, S. "Cosmological Signs in Calculating the Time of Redemption: The Christian Crucifixion and the New Moon of Nissan." *Viator* 35 (2004): 265–87.

Sharot, S. *Messianism, Mysticism, and Magic: A Sociological Analysis of Jewish Religious Movements.* Chapel Hill: 1982.

Shatzmiller. J. "Les Angevins et les Juifs de leurs états: Anjou, Naples et Provence." In *L' Etat Angevin: pouvior, culture, et société entre XIIIe et XIVe siècle.* Rome: 1998.

Silver, D. J. *Maimonidean Criticism and the Maimonidean Controversy 1180–1240.* Leiden: 1965.

Simonsohn, S. *The Jews in Sicily,* Vol. 1 (383–1300). Leiden: 1997.

Sirat, C. *A History of Jewish Philosophy in the Middle Ages.* Cambridge: 1985.

Starr, J. "The Mass Conversions of Jews in Southern Italy (1290–1293)." *Speculum* 21 (1946): 203–11.

Steinschneider, M. "Outline for the Life of Zerahiah b. Shaltiel Hen" (Hebrew). *Ozar Nechmad* 2 (1857): 229–45.

———. *Hebraeischen Ubersetzungen des Mittelalters.* Berlin: 1893.

Stern, D., and M. J. Mirsky, eds. *Rabbinic Fantasies: Imaginative Narratives from Classical Hebrew Literature.* New Haven and London: 1990.

Tocci, F. M. "Dottrine 'Eremetich' tra gli ebrei in Italia fino al Cinqucento." In *Italia Judaica: Atti del 1 Convegno internazionali Bari 18–22 Maggio 1981.* Rome: 1983.

Tolan, J. *Petrus Alfonsi and His Medieval Readers.* Gainesville: 1993.

Töpfer, B. *Il regno futuro della libertà.* Genoa: 1992.

Traver, A. G. "The *Liber de Antichristo* and the Failure of Joachite Expectations." *Florensia* 15 (2001): 87–98.

Vogelstein, H. *A History of the Jews in Rome.* Philadelphia: 1940.

———, and P. Rieger. *Geschichte der Juden in Rom.* 2 Vols. Berlin: 1896.

Wannenmacher, J. E. *Hermeneutik der Heilsgeschichte. De septem sigillis und die sieben Siegel im Werk Joachims von Fiore.* Leiden: 2005.

Wasserstrom, S. M. *Between Muslim and Jew: The Problem of Symbiosis under Early Islam.* Princeton: 1995.

Weber, E. *Apocalypses: Prophecies, Cults, and Millenial Beliefs through the Ages.* Toronto: 1999.

Wessley, S. E. *Joachim of Fiore and Monastic Reform*. New York: 1990.

———. 'The Role of the Holy Land for the Early Followers of Joachim of Fiore." In *The Holy Land, Holy Lands, and Christian History* (*Studies in Church History* 36), ed. R. N. Swanson. Rochester: 2000.

———. "The True and New Jews: Jerusalem Rebuilt." *Frate Francesco: Rivisti de cultura francescana* n.s. 70, no. 2 (2004): 285–314.

West, D. C. *Joachimism and Fra Salimbene*. PhD thesis, UCLA. Los Angeles: 1970.

———. 'Between Flesh and Spirit: Joachite Pattern and Meaning in the Cronica of Fra Salimbene." *Journal of Medieval History* 3, no. 4 (1977): 339–52.

———. "The Education of Fra Salimbene of Parma: the Joachite Influence." In *Prophecy and Millenarianism: Essays in Honour of Marjorie Reeves,* ed. A. Williams. London: 1980.

Wirszubski, C. "Liber Redemptionis—the Early Version of R. Abraham Abulafia's Kabbalistic *Commentary on the Guide for the Perplexed* in the Latin Translation of Flavius Mithridates." *Divri ha-Akedemia ha-Leumit le-Ma'daim* 3. Jerusalem: 1970.

———. *Pico della Mirandola's Encounter with Jewish Mysticism*. Cambridge, MA: 1989.

Wolfson, E. "By Way of Truth: Aspects of Nahmanides' Kabbalistic Hermeneutic." *Association of Jewish Studies Review* 14 (1989): 103–78.

———. *Abraham Abulafia—Kabbalist and Prophet: Hermeneutics, Theosophy, and Theurgy*. Los Angeles: 2000.

Yuval, I. J. "Jewish Messianic Expectations towards 1240 and Christian Reaction." In *Toward the Millenium: Messianic Expectations from the Bible to Waco,* ed. P. Schäfer and M. Cohen. Leiden: 1998.

———. *"Two Nations in Your Womb": Perceptions of Jews and Christians in Late Antiquity and the Middle Ages.* Berkeley and Los Angeles: 2006.

Index